unicef🌐

A school like mine

A unique celebration of schools around the world

How A School Like Mine is helping children get back to school

" *The United Nations Children's Fund, or* **UNICEF** *for short, does amazing work to help children all over the world. One of their many projects is to send mini schools to places that have been devastated by disasters including floods and earthquakes. Each school fits neatly into a suitcase-sized box and is called a* **School-in-a-Box.**

In 2005 I was lucky enough to help pack **School-in-a-Box** *kits after the Asian Tsunami. These were sent to teachers who set up classrooms wherever they could, usually outside. Then children who had lost everything could at least have the stability of a school to go to while their own was being rebuilt.*

Tsunami in Sri Lanka, 2005

For every copy of A School Like Mine *that's sold an average of 75¢ goes to* **UNICEF** *to buy more* **School-in-a-Box** *kits. So when you buy a copy of this book, you are helping to educate children around the world and give them the chance of a brighter future.*

Thank you very much for helping to make a difference. "

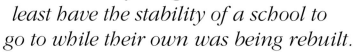

David Beckham
Goodwill Ambassador
for **UNICEF**

What's in the box?

School-in-a-Box kits are packed with things you would normally find in a classroom—exercise books, pencils, erasers, and scissors. These fit neatly inside a lockable metal box. Each kit has enough materials and supplies for a teacher and up to 80 students.

The lid of the box can be coated with a special paint and used as a blackboard.

Setting up school
This **School-in-a-Box** was sent to the district of Galle in southern Sri Lanka, where these children's school was damaged during the tsunami. One hundred children, including six from this class, were killed during the disaster. Their regular school was reopened in January 2006.

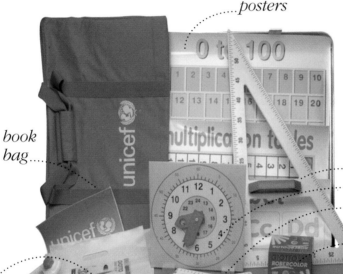

posters

triangle

teaching clock

rulers

white chalks

colored cubes

crayons

exercise books

colored chalks

blackboard eraser

drawing slate

book bag

pencils

giant compass

adhesive tape

safety scissors

large scissors

measuring tape

pens

blackboard paint

paintbrush

pencil sharpener

Eager to learn
These preschool children in Liberia are just a handful of the millions who have benefited from **School-in-a-Box**. The children are in a temporary learning space set up by UNICEF to ensure a safe and child-friendly place where children are free to learn.

A box full of hope

If you want to know more about **School-in-a-Box** and UNICEF's other projects, or to make a donation, visit **www.unicef.org**

DK

LONDON, NEW YORK, MUNICH,
MELBOURNE, and DELHI

Written and edited by Penny Smith
and Zahavit Shalev
Designed by Sonia Whillock-Moore
Additional editing Caroline Bingham,
Elinor Greenwood, Carrie Love,
Lorrie Mack, and Fleur Star
US Editor Margaret Parrish
Additional design Gemma Fletcher, Tory
Gordon-Harris, Karen Hood,
Poppy Joslin, and Sadie Thomas
Publishing Manager Susan Leonard
Managing Art Editor Rachael Foster
DTP designer Ben Hung
Production Lucy Baker
Jacket designer Sadie Thomas
Photographers Bryan Alexander,
Frank Chen, Andy Crawford,
Howard Davies, George Fetting, Steve
Gorton, Minnie Pang Walker, Simon
Rawles, Joginder Singh, and Jon Spaull
UNICEF Consultant Heather Jarvis

First American Edition, 2007

First published in the United States by
DK Publishing Inc.
375 Hudson Street
New York, NY 10014

07 08 09 10 11 10 9 8 7 6 5 4 3 2 1
AD358—04/07

Copyright © 2007 Dorling Kindersley Limited

All rights reserved under International and Pan-American
Copyright Conventions. No part of this publication may be
reproduced, stored in a retrieval system, or transmitted in
any form or by any means, electronic, mechanical,
photocopying, recording, or otherwise, without the prior
written permission of the copyright owner. Published in
Great Britain by Dorling Kindersley Limited.

A catalog record for this book is available from
the Library of Congress.

ISBN 978-0-7566-2913-7

Color reproduction by MDP, UK
Printed and bound by TBB, Slovakia

Carbon emissions from flights undertaken to make
this book have been offset through Climate Care.

Discover more at **www.dk.com**

Contents

8 The Americas

10 Maria from Peru
12 Yasmin from Brazil
13 Ana from Brazil
14 Jucari from Mexico
16 Carmen from Mexico
18 Emmy from the US
20 Ian from the US
21 Sander from the US
22 Lukasi from Canada

24 Africa

26 Fundi from South Africa
27 Sibusiso from South Africa
28 Safaa from Egypt
30 Semira from Ethiopia
32 Susan from Botswana

Meet the children

Visiting schools in six continents (out of a world total of seven) has meant a lot of traveling! And at each destination children have been busily learning their languages, practicing math, and playing ball at recess. What's amazing is how similar schools are—and also the fascinating differences. So now it's time to meet the children from schools all around the world.

CANADA • Kuujjuaq

NORTH AMERICA

UNITED STATES

• Boston

Bonny Dune •

• Houston

MEXICO

• Aguascalientes
• Mexico City

PERU

BRAZIL

Huaraz •

SOUTH AMERICA

• Rio de Janeiro

I'm Maria and I'm from Peru

I'm Yasmin and I'm from Brazil

I'm Ana and I'm from Brazil

From the Americas

I'm Jucari and I'm from Mexico

I'm Carmen and I'm from Mexico

I'm Emmy and I'm from the US

I'm Ian and I'm from the US

I'm Sander and I'm from the US

I'm Lukasi and I'm from Canada

I'm Dana and I'm from Jordan

I'm Yotam and I'm from Israel

From Africa

I'm Fundi and I'm from South Africa

I'm Sibusiso and I'm from South Africa

I'm Safaa and I'm from Egypt

I'm Semira and I'm from Ethiopia

I'm Susan and I'm from Botswana

From Europe

I'm Francis and I'm from England

I'm Michael and I'm from Ireland

I'm Gapirri and I'm from Australia

I'm Parekaawa and I'm from New Zealand

From Asia

I'm Ksenia and I'm from the Russian Federation

I'm Alexei and I'm from the Russian Federation

I'm Aysima and I'm from Turkey

We're Deepak and Atul; we're from India

I'm Sumandhara and I'm from India

I'm Reena and I'm from India

I'm Xinpei and I'm from China

I'm Jiyu and I'm from China

I'm Yiting and I'm from China

I'm Hassa and I'm from Mongolia

I'm Sun-Woo and I'm from South Korea

I'm Momona and I'm from Japan

I'm Junivio and I'm from East Timor

I'm Anna and I'm from France

We're Nacho and Alvaro and we're from Spain

I'm Flora and I'm from Belgium

I'm Isabelle and I'm from the Netherlands

I'm Søren and I'm from Denmark

I'm Chiara and I'm from Italy

I'm Fanny and I'm from Germany

I'm Marek and I'm from Poland

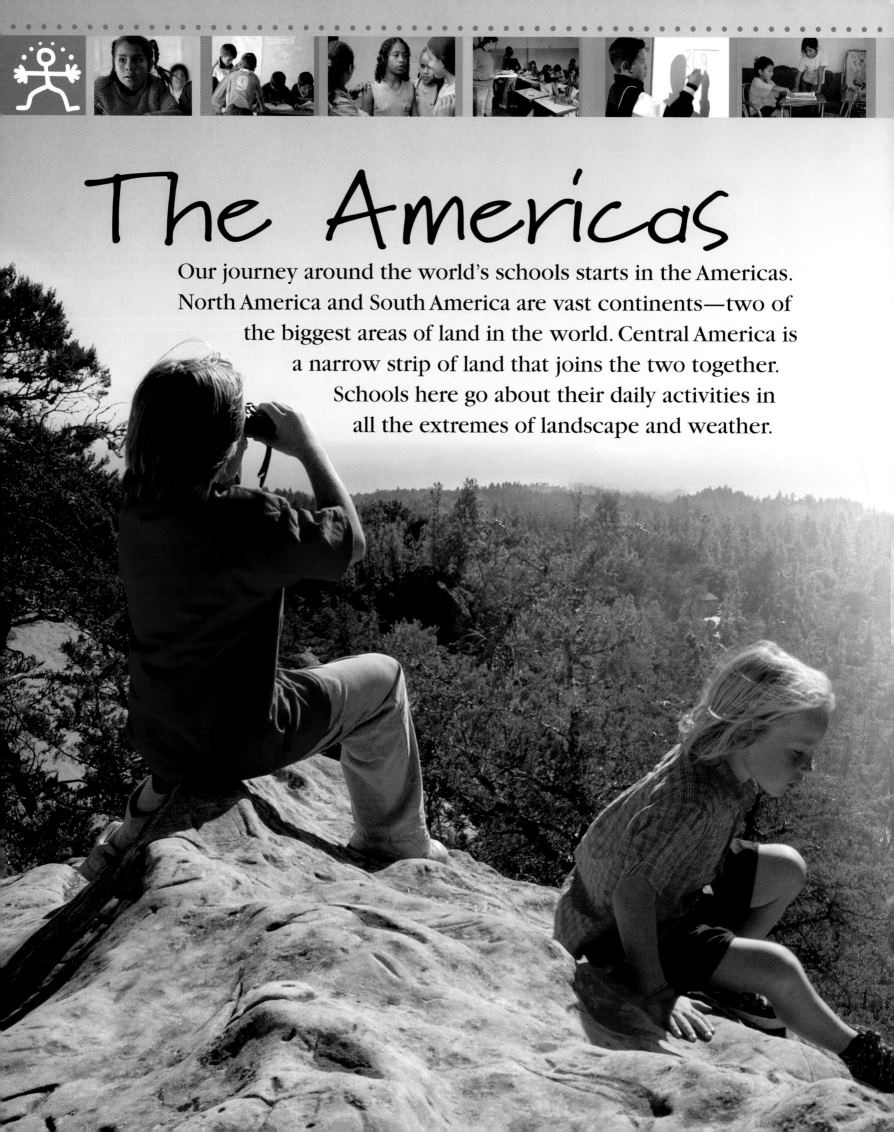

The Americas

Our journey around the world's schools starts in the Americas. North America and South America are vast continents—two of the biggest areas of land in the world. Central America is a narrow strip of land that joins the two together. Schools here go about their daily activities in all the extremes of landscape and weather.

This is North America and South America

Northern Canada

Sometimes the best way to get around Canada's far north, where the temperature can dip to as low as -40°F (-40°C), is by dog sled.

Hockey, Canada

Hockey is the top sport in Canada—and many children play it at school. Protective clothing must be worn, since players may collide (called "checking"), and the puck can travel at 100 mph (160 km/h) if it's hit hard.

Capital city

The capital city of the United States of America is Washington, D.C.—and the Capitol building is where Congress meets to pass laws and engage in other official matters.

California

Sandy beaches, snow-capped mountains, cultured cities, national parks, Hollywood, Disneyland... California has it all.

The Grand Canyon

The US has some spectacular scenery, including the colorful rocks of the Grand Canyon. In some places, the Grand Canyon is more than a mile (1.6 km) deep.

Mexico

Mexico is in North America and its official language is Spanish—there are more Spanish speakers here than in Spain. The countryside varies from desert to mountain, with beaches along both coasts.

Brazil

Brazil is the largest country in South America and home to the Amazon rain forest. Every year, in the city of Rio de Janeiro, the world-famous Rio Carnival is held.

Peru

The world's longest chain of mountains, the Andes, covers nearly half of Peru. Machu Picchu (left), an ancient ruined city of the Incas, is situated high up in the peaks. Many different native peoples live in Peru, both in the Andes and in the Amazon Basin, which covers the rest of the country.

Map labels:

GREENLAND (To Denmark)

ALASKA (United States)

CANADA

NORTH AMERICA

UNITED STATES

Kuujjuaq

Bonny Dune

Boston

MEXICO

Houston

BAHAMAS

CUBA

DOMINICAN REPUBLIC

HAITI

Aguascalientes

Mexico City

BELIZE JAMAICA

GUATEMALA HONDURAS

EL SALVADOR NICARAGUA

COSTA RICA

PANAMA

VENEZUELA

GUYANA

SURINAM

FRENCH GUIANA (To France)

COLOMBIA

ECUADOR

PERU

Huaraz

BRAZIL

SOUTH AMERICA

BOLIVIA

PARAGUAY

Rio de Janeiro

CHILE

ARGENTINA

URUGUAY

FALKLAND ISLANDS (To UK)

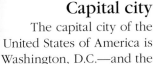

Maria from Peru

Maria lives in Pampacancha, a village in the Andes region of Peru. Most people here live off the food they grow. Maria's parents are separated. Her mother lives and works in the town of Huaraz, 30 miles (50 km) away.

Pampacancha nestles in the Cordillera Negra—the black mountains—where rain and snow rarely fall.

This young puppy doesn't yet have a name.

Family

Maria and her brother Eliseo live with their grandmother, two aunts, an uncle, and two young cousins.

Education for everyone

The government is encouraging rural families to keep their children at school rather than employ them at home. This mural at Maria's school says: "Girls and boys have the right to study."

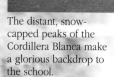

The distant, snow-capped peaks of the Cordillera Blanca make a glorious backdrop to the school.

At 10, Maria is older than the rest of her class because she is making up the year of school she missed when she lived in Huaraz with her mother.

Languages

Maria has copied out the words of a Quechua-language song. Schools in Peru used to teach only in Spanish, but Quechua children often couldn't keep up and would drop out. Now, children learn in both languages.

wara
Pants

ruripa
Skirt

Warmipa Tsukun
Man's hat

Ullqupa Tsukun
Woman's hat

A bite to eat

At midmorning break the children are given soy milk and fortified bread (bread with added vitamins), provided by the government. This is their first meal of the day.

Fortified bread

Food is one good reason why children attend school.

Everyone crowds around the school's first and only computer. They are all excited about having a computer to use.

Outdoor lessons

Sometimes the teacher takes the class outside for a nature lesson. This is a chance to learn practical things, such as how to plant and tend crops, or the best way to care for the domestic animals like sheep, cows, and hens that people rely on.

A close-up look at a chicken.

"...Today I used a computer for the first time. It was exciting! The computer uses Spanish, but normally we use Quechua in class."

There's no sports equipment, but the children play games such as tug-of-war and leapfrog.

These children are getting ready for a wheelbarrow race.

Helping out

After school, Maria and Eliseo help their grandmother to pick wheat for the main meal. They then use the water from this standpipe to wash the wheat and remove the chaff. Later, Maria helps her aunt to do some laundry.

Day-to-day

Maria's school is just minutes from her home. When she goes to junior high school, Maria will have to walk a steep mountain track to the next town. It will take an hour downhill every morning and two hours to walk back up every afternoon.

Yasmin from Brazil

Eleven-year-old Yasmin lives in a poor neighborhood of Rio de Janeiro. There are 32 children in her class and not enough teachers to go around. There are no computers for the students to use.

School days
Lessons start at 7:30 a.m. and usually end at noon, but sometimes Yasmin has to go home early if there is no teacher for her class.

Family life
Yasmin has four brothers and three sisters. The children's grandmother looks after them while their mother is at work.

Yasmin and her mother share a love of teddy bears.

Making learning fun
A 15-year-old student at the school reads a story to Yasmin's class. The goal of these classes is to encourage the children's interest in reading.

Yasmin really enjoys her drumming class. They play a kind of Brazilian music called samba. Huge groups of hundreds of drummers perform at the Rio Carnival.

" *...My favorite lesson is English. It's important to speak other languages.* "

Lunch today is pasta and sausages.

Lunchtime
A free meal is provided for the children. Usually it's beans and rice, chicken with potatoes, or pasta and sausages.

The school runs dance classes for the community.

Yasmin plays in the courtyard outside her home.

Yasmin and her sister wash the dishes after lunch.

Ana from Brazil

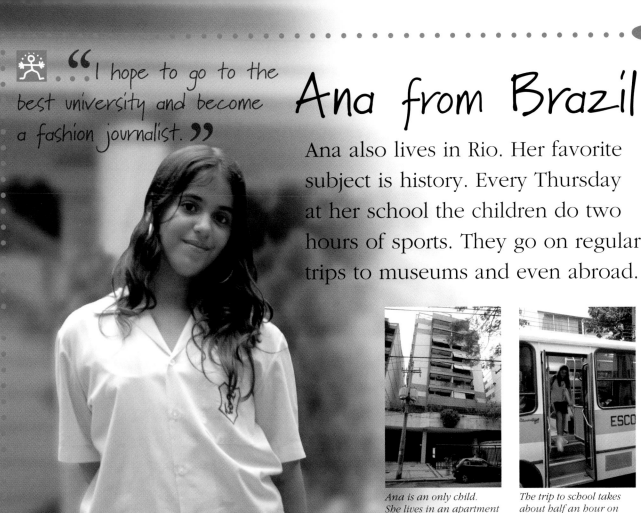

Ana also lives in Rio. Her favorite subject is history. Every Thursday at her school the children do two hours of sports. They go on regular trips to museums and even abroad.

Ana is an only child. She lives in an apartment with her parents.

The trip to school takes about half an hour on the bus.

Helping others

Ana is fortunate to attend a spacious school. Pupils there raise money for a center that provides poor children with a place to study, eat a hot meal, and sleep. Twice a year they visit the center to play with the children who use it.

Ana goes to regular street-dancing lessons. She has been attending classes since she was five and although she still enjoys them, she's starting to get a little bored now.

The latest technology

The school is well equipped with computers. The students use them a great deal for lessons and tests.

Ana's English language textbook

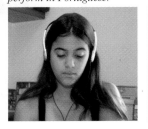
One of Ana's ceramic dolls and an RBD CD

Ana likes to listen to RBD, a Mexican band that also perform in Portuguese.

After she does her homework, Ana surfs the net on the computer in her bedroom.

Ana and her mother chat in the kitchen. The family has a maid to do the cleaning.

Jucari from Mexico

Jucari, who is ten, lives with his mother, father, and six-year-old sister in a residential area of Mexico City. His family was originally Purepecha Indian, and his name means "great wise one" in their language. Jucari goes to a large public school in the center of the city.

Jucari says goodbye to his mother at the school gates. Although his trip should take about an hour, it takes twice as long when the traffic is very heavy.

School life

The school's courtyard provides a big, safe place for Jucari and his friends to play before classes and at recess. The boys and girls at their school all wear a comfortable blue and white uniform and sneakers.

... "I would like to be an archeologist and study old temples. "

Daily classes

Jucari pays attention during math class, but his favorite subject is history. There are 36 children in his class, and their teacher is Fernando Miranda. They call him *maestro* Fernando.

Jucari chose his desk because it is close to both the blackboard and the interactive whiteboard. There are plenty of computers in the school, and Jucari enjoys using them.

Jucari's notebook is full of cars.

This is his math book.

Day of the Dead

In Mexico, the Day of the Dead is an important celebration. On this day, people ask the spirits to look after them in their everyday lives. Jucari places an offering of sweets on the school altar before a portrait of Benito Juárez, a Mexican president who fought to ensure schooling for every child.

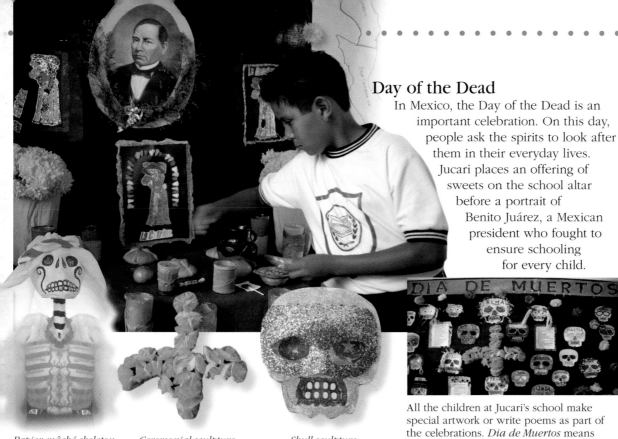

Papier-mâché skeleton　　*Ceremonial sculpture*　　*Skull sculpture*

All the children at Jucari's school make special artwork or write poems as part of the celebrations. *Dia de Muertos* means Day of the Dead in Spanish.

After school

With his mother, Jucari takes the subway home from school. Then they take the car or catch the bus, to either his house or to the candy store his mother owns.

Jucari and his mother squeeze onto a rush-hour train. Every day he gets homework, which he carries in his backpack.

Jucari and his sister often eat at their grandfather's. His tailoring business is next door to their mother's candy store.

Jucari sleeps in a race-car bed. He loves race cars, but he doesn't want to drive one because they're dangerous.

Recess

Jucari's favorite playground game is *Tazos*™, which is played with tokens found in bags of potato chips and snacks. Each player puts a token on the ground, then his opponents try to flip it over with their own tokens. Whoever succeeds keeps both tokens.

Children can't buy Tazos™ in stores—they have to collect them from potato chip bags or win them from their friends.

Jucari and his sister have a cat, and it's Jucari's job to feed it and clean its box.

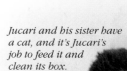

The school has its own outdoor swimming pool.

School sports

Jucari enjoys lots of sports at school, including track events, basketball, soccer, swimming, and handball—he is on the school handball team.

Carmen from Mexico

Carmen is the youngest of 14 children, whose ages range from 36 down to 10. She lives in a tiny village in the state of Aguascalientes in Mexico. The school she goes to has just nine pupils, who are all taught together by their instructor, Michaela, who recently left high school.

Carmen and her mother near their home with one of Carmen's nieces and one of her nephews. Although her family is very large, this is not unheard of in rural areas of Mexico.

The school
The building on the left was the schoolroom until the new building on the right was built.

Carmen's model of a traditional Mexican house

Carmen's favorite teddy bear

Carmen with her class. Their instructor is at the back with "16" on her top.

... Sometimes we get science experiments to do at home using things like plants, nails, oil, salt, and matches. **

Children attend school from 8 a.m. to 1:30 p.m., Monday to Friday. Maria does 30 minutes of homework each day, too.

The school has a computer.

Children's art decorates the school walls.

Day-to-day
There is not enough money to pay for teachers in all rural areas. Therefore, young people who have just finished high school are allowed to teach for a couple of years. In return, they receive a free college education.

Herb garden

The children grow herbs in the schoolyard. People here grow much of their own food and children are expected to help.

Math book

The Mexican government supplies small rural schools with textbooks designed for children learning in mixed age groups. Carmen works through her book at her own pace with help from the instructor.

Carmen and one of her classmates doing a math exercise outside their school. Their instructor works hard to make learning active and fun.

Schedule of jobs for the children

Chores

The children take an active role in looking after their school. Every child has a different job each day, such as collecting water or mopping the floor, as Carmen is doing here.

Field trip

Carmen loves natural sciences because this class offers an opportunity to go out and explore. In fact, a great deal of learning takes place outside the classroom. The children have interviewed local elderly people and visited the river to learn about caring for the environment.

Making meals

There are no local stores. Instead, a truck comes around selling fruit and vegetables to the villagers.

Carmen helps her mother to cook a typical dinner—noodle soup with tomatoes, onions, and peppers accompanied by a chili salsa and corn tortillas.

Afterward, Carmen washes the dishes using a large bucket, which she fills from the faucet outside the house.

Carmen plays at being a school instructor with her nephew.

Houston is the fourth largest city in the United States. The city is probably best known for being the home of the NASA Space Program, which was set up to discover more about space.

Emmy from the US

Nine-year-old Emmy lives very close to her school in the suburbs of Houston, Texas. She likes to cycle to school, a trip of about three minutes, but sometimes takes the bus. Emmy's school works with the community and at Christmas arranges for the children to take gifts, clothes, and food to low-income families.

The neighborhood

There is plenty of land in the suburbs so the family home has a front- and backyard. This is a very friendly community. Emmy spends her free time with her friends at the neighborhood pool and playground. Every year the local families get together to organize a street party.

Emmy with her parents, brother, Andrew, and sister, Caroline

The sign on Emmy's bedroom door

Caroline & Emmy's Room

Soccer Princess

Sharing a room

Emmy shares a room with her older sister Caroline, who is 12. One wall is almost completely covered with photographs of the girls' friends.

The wall of photos in the girls' bedroom.

Emmy was in kindergarten when she drew this picture of her mother.

Flying the flag

The school's flagpole displays two flags—the flag of the United States, nicknamed the "Stars and Stripes," and the state flag for Texas, the "Lone Star Flag." Every morning there is a short ceremony by the flagpole and the children say the Pledge of Allegiance to both flags.

Emmy's school is on the same street as her home. This is the schoolyard inside the school gates at the front of the school.

There is a large playground at the back of the school for recess, with plenty of trees to provide shade during the hot summer months.

Church

Emmy's family is Greek Orthodox Christian. Houston is home to one of the biggest Greek Orthodox communities in the United States. Every October the community hosts the "Original Greek Festival"—three days of Greek food, music, and dance. It has been a regular event in Houston for the past 40 years.

Emmy plays sports through the church and other youth groups.

Class trips

There are 20 children in Emmy's class, made up of an equal number of girls and boys. Last year they saw a production at the Houston Ballet. This year, they are looking forward to a bus trip to visit the state capital, Austin. Emmy started here at the age of four and will go to middle school when she is 11.

Emmy draws flowers in her art class.

In the classroom, Emmy sits at one of five desks pushed together.

There is no uniform, but the school does not allow tank tops or very short shorts.

Avid sportswoman

Emmy swims competitively and would like to be a professional swimmer when she grows up. She and her friends play kickball and four square in the school playground, and she also plays basketball, softball, and volleyball outside of school.

A school day

The school day runs from 8 a.m. to 3 p.m., Monday to Friday. All the classes are in English. Emmy loves learning in groups and using the computer. Her least favorite subjects are music and math.

The school has a computer lab and there are also computers in some of the classrooms.

Emmy rehearses for a performance of the ballet, The Nutcracker.

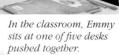

At recess, Emmy and her friends play a game called four square.

Ian from the US

Ian lives in Boston. Most days his dad gives him a ride to school in the car, which takes about 10 minutes, but sometimes he walks with his mom. He likes everything about his school.

On his way to school, Ian likes to look out for children he knows from the local high school, where his dad is the athletics director.

Ian is an only child.

He plays lots of sports.

Baseball

Ian loves sports, and would like to become a professional baseball player. His bedroom is full of sports memorabilia, but there is still room for his pet guinea pig's cage.

Baseball trophy

This is Peanut, Ian's pet guinea pig.

Ian is an accomplished pianist and takes lessons at the Community Music Center. His father plays in a heavy metal band.

School days

School runs from 8 a.m. to 3:15 p.m., Monday to Friday. Ian is now 10, and he started here when he was six. He'll be 12 when he leaves.

In the classroom

There are 17 children in Ian's class. Ian likes to sit in the middle of the room facing the door, but he doesn't sit in the same place every day.

This is an illustrated story Ian wrote himself.

Lunchtime

Everybody brings a sack lunch. Ian's mother makes his and then checks if it's OK with him. It always is.

Some children play soccer in the school playground, while others sit on the sidelines and cheer them on.

Sander from the US

Sander is eleven and lives in Bonny Dune, California. He spends three days a week being homeschooled by his parents, with his brother, Olin, and two days a week at school. He likes learning at his own pace.

Feeding the chickens and collecting their eggs is Sander's job.

Nature report

Sander chose this Ponderosa Pine for his nature report. He and his dad used a special tool to cut a tiny core out of the tree to help them calculate its age.

The tree rings suggest that this pine is from 300 to 400 years old.

The boys and their father make a picture to celebrate Halloween. Later, Sander practices the violin. Sander's parents each take turns teaching Sander and Olin.

Sander's exercise book

Baseball dreams

Sander plays in a baseball league during the fall and winter. He would love to become a professional player.

Baseball trophy

At school the children don't sit at desks but around tables. There are different work stations for each subject.

The boys bake a pumpkin pie as part of a cooking lesson with their father.

A glove worn by Alex Rodriguez of the New York Yankees

Sander owns a signed baseball.

The forest is a few minutes' drive away.

Free time

California's climate is mild, so Sander spends a lot of time playing outdoors.

He loves skateboarding and skates whenever he can.

The boys play in a tree house Sander made.

Sander dug this fort, which is deep enough to stand in.

Tubbs, the family cat

Lukasi from Canada

Ten-year-old Lukasi lives in Kuujjuaq, the largest Inuit village in Quebec, Canada. Conditions can be extreme. Daytime winter temperatures average about -18°F (-28°C), and that's without the wind! Summers are mild at around 52°F (11°C).

Kuujjuaq is so remote that there are no roads linking it with anywhere else. People can only travel in and out by air or sea.

In midwinter it's dark for 20 hours a day.

Lukasi is very used to eating his breakfast cereal in the dark.

Arctic village

About 2,000 people live in Kuujjuaq. Most of them are Inuit and their first language is Inuktitut. Quebec has two official languages, English and French, so Lukasi can speak these languages, too. The village is the transportation hub for the whole region, so as well as stores and restaurants it also has an airport with two runways.

Snowmobiles are the best vehicles for riding on snow. They are like motorcycles, but with skis.

Traditional Inuit sealskin boots, called *kamiks,* hang on hooks by the door. No modern fiber can match sealskin for keeping feet warm and dry in the Arctic cold.

In his spare time Lukasi loves to go hunting, fishing, and trapping, just as his ancestors did.

This dog belongs to Lukasi's grandfather. She is named Mala because she is an Alaskan Malamute. A thick coat protects her from the cold.

Lukasi and his two sisters, Amelia, 13, and Qullik, five, stay with their grandparents when their parents have to go away for work.

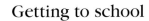

Getting to school
Lukasi lives close to his school, so it's rare for him to stay home because of bad weather. He can walk to school in 10 minutes. He often meets dogs along the way that he likes to stop and pet.

Some of the children travel into school on a bright yellow school bus. It makes a circuit of about 5 miles (8 km) to pick everybody up. Occasionally school is canceled because of a storm, but it is never closed because of cold weather.

*...*I speak Inuktitut, French, and English. I don't like Inuktitut class because the girls bug the boys.*

Lukasi is very athletic. Here he plays dodgeball with the kids in his class. Lukasi also plays soccer, tennis, and badminton.

The view from Lukasi's classroom

A plaque in traditional Inuit style

My class
There are 18 children in Lukasi's class—five boys and 13 girls—and their ages range from eight to 12. They don't have to wear a school uniform. Lukasi sits at his own desk, but some children share.

Homework takes about 20 minutes each night.

Lukasi makes notes about an experiment he is doing in science class. His homework will be about the experiment.

Karate class
Lukasi has been doing karate since he was seven years old. About 25 children in Kuujjuaq attend karate lessons twice a week. Lukasi likes karate, but his favorite hobbies are hunting, fishing, and trapping.

Waiting to begin. *Doing stretches to warm up.* *Preparing for a high kick!*

With help from his grandfather, Lukasi makes a Samurai sword out of wood. His grandfather ordered the wood from Montreal and it arrived by ship in the summer. Over the years they have made medieval swords and shields as well as hunting rifles together.

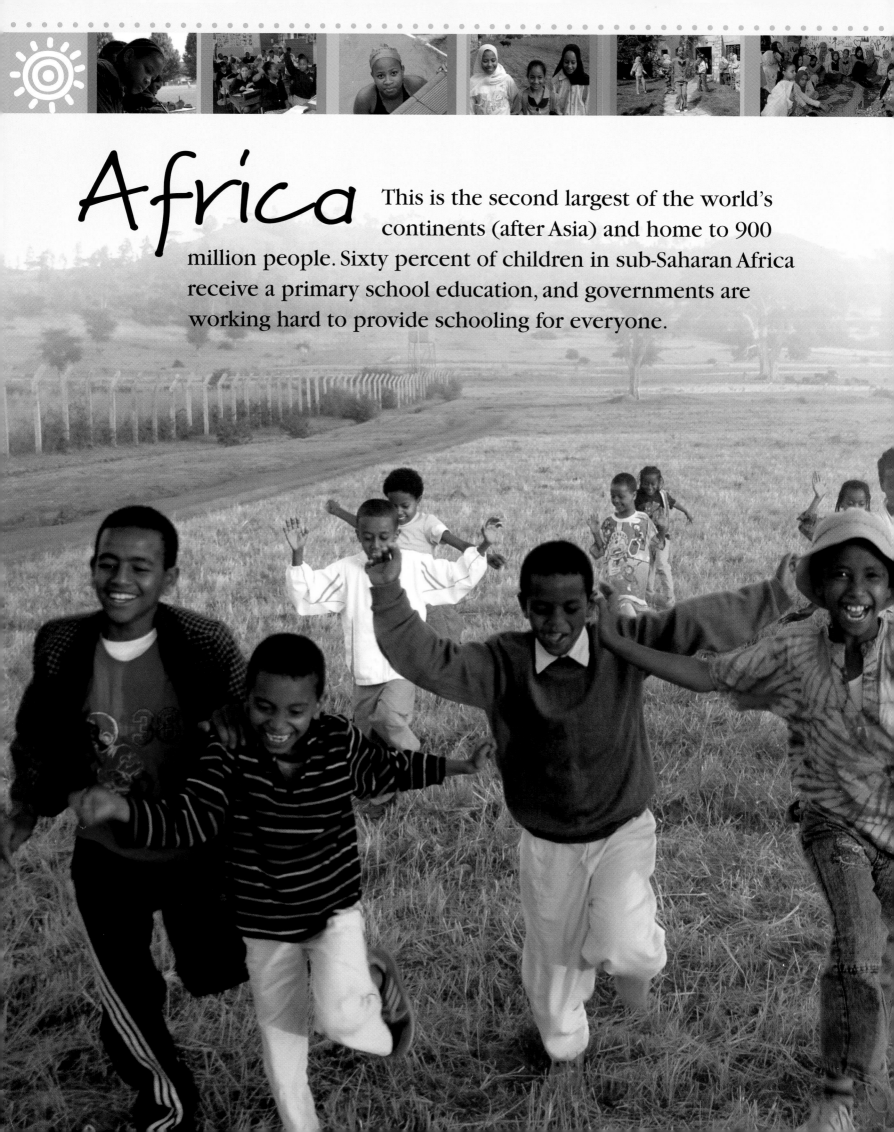

Africa

This is the second largest of the world's continents (after Asia) and home to 900 million people. Sixty percent of children in sub-Saharan Africa receive a primary school education, and governments are working hard to provide schooling for everyone.

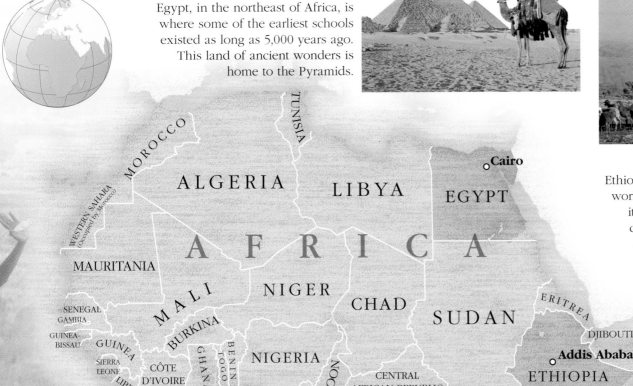

This is Africa

Egypt

Egypt, in the northeast of Africa, is where some of the earliest schools existed as long as 5,000 years ago. This land of ancient wonders is home to the Pyramids.

Ethiopia

Ethiopia is one of the oldest nations in the world, and unlike other African countries it managed, largely, to avoid European colonization. At least 70 languages are spoken in Ethiopia, but English is the main foreign language, since it is the one teachers use in high schools.

MOROCCO
WESTERN SAHARA (Occupied by Morocco)
TUNISIA
ALGERIA
LIBYA
EGYPT
Cairo
MAURITANIA
AFRICA
MALI
NIGER
CHAD
SUDAN
SENEGAL
GAMBIA
GUINEA-BISSAU
GUINEA
BURKINA
BENIN
TOGO
NIGERIA
ERITREA
DJIBOUTI
SIERRA LEONE
CÔTE D'IVOIRE
GHANA
CAMEROON
CENTRAL AFRICAN REPUBLIC
Addis Ababa
ETHIOPIA
SOMALIA
LIBERIA
EQUATORIAL GUINEA
GABON
CONGO
DEMOCRATIC REPUBLIC OF THE CONGO
UGANDA
RWANDA
BURUNDI
KENYA
TANZANIA
ANGOLA
ZAMBIA
MALAWI
MOZAMBIQUE
MADAGASCAR
NAMIBIA
ZIMBABWE
BOTSWANA
Molepolole
SWAZILAND
SOUTH AFRICA
LESOTHO
Richmond

Botswana

Botswana is landlocked, and despite the Kalahari Desert in the west, it is a haven for wildlife. Crocodiles, buffalo, wildebeest, lions, hippos, rhinos, giraffe, and the African elephant are all found here.

South African landscape

The South African landscape varies from the dry Karoo interior to the many gardens and vineyards of the Cape. Cape Town, the capital (shown here), sits below the spectacular cliffs of the flat-topped Table Mountain, here shrouded in cloud, nicknamed the "tablecloth."

Wildlife in South Africa

South Africa is home to the "big five"—buffalo, elephant, leopard, lion, and rhino. The coastal waters teem with sea creatures, and a huge variety of birds, including Jackass penguins, make their homes here.

Fundi from South Africa

Fundi is 12 years old and goes to boarding school in Richmond, South Africa. She spends three weeks at a time there, then goes home to see her family.

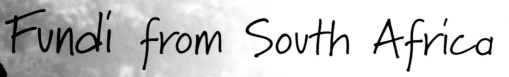

☀ 66 My hero is Nelson Mandela, first president of the new South Africa. 99

Nelson Mandela fought against apartheid, which separated people because of their race.

In summer Fundi wears a navy blue and white dress. In winter she wears a navy suit.

Fundi wears white socks in summer and navy socks in winter.

Pietermaritzburg

Fundi's school is spread over sloping hills on the outskirts of the town of Richmond. Nearby is the city of Pietermaritzburg, where many students from Fundi's school will go to high school.

Start the day

Fundi wakes up at 6 a.m. and has eggs and traditional oatmeal for breakfast. She usually wears a school uniform, but on Market Day she can wear her own clothes.

The school system

Fundi has a different teacher for each subject and she likes them all. This is Miss Mkhize, who teaches Zulu and netball. There are 27 children in Fundi's class and almost half of them are boarders.

On Market Day, Fundi and her friends sell food they have made themselves as part of their schoolwork. They have to keep track of costs so they can make a profit when they sell the food.

Dormitory life

Fundi shares a dormitory with nine other girls. They are not allowed to talk after lights out at 8:30 p.m. and sometimes Fundi finds it hard to go right to sleep.

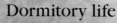

After school, Fundi and her friends meet at a bench on the school grounds. It's their chance to catch up and share stories. Fundi likes having boys in her school because she thinks they are fun.

Sports days

Fundi plays sports most days. Her school has a swimming pool and she likes swimming there, even in chilly weather. Fundi is on the school swim team. The school also teaches cricket and soccer, but only the boys play these.

Fundi is good at netball. She is on the school team, which competes against other schools.

In the computer room, children play games, make spreadsheets, and learn how to type.

"*I'd like to be a pilot when I grow up.*"

Sibusiso from South Africa

Eleven-year-old Sibusiso lives on a strawberry farm outside Richmond in South Africa. His home is 5 miles (8 km) from school and each day it takes him over an hour to walk there.

The long walk
Although it is tiring, Sibusiso doesn't mind the walk to school. He is on his own for half the trip, then he meets friends and they walk the rest of the way together.

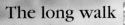
Sibusiso tries to keep his math book neat.

To keep safe, children walk in single file by the road. The child in front carries a flag.

A working day
When Sibusiso leaves for school, his father goes to work on the farm and his mother sets off to her job in the farm owner's kitchen.

Sibusiso's parents work on a strawberry farm like this one.

Sibusiso drew this picture of the farm owner's house. This is where he goes to watch television.

School age
There are 23 children in Sibusiso's class. They are mostly the same age as Sibusiso, although some, who missed out on their early education, are as old as 15.

Sibusiso's school bag is a backpack that he carries on his back.

Classrooms open onto the playground. Sometimes the children have an outdoor assembly on the grass.

Children grow plants in the school garden. It is fenced in with barbed wire to keep robbers out of the school buildings.

Miss Priscilla Reddy is the principal.

This sign is on the library door. Its message is that the school does not tolerate violence of any kind.

Rice and stew is a typical school meal.
The cook serves food from the veranda of her house.
The children eat lunch on benches outside their classrooms.

School lunch
Sibusiso enjoys the food that is cooked at school. Like the other children, he washes and dries his plate after the meal.

Cairo

The largest city in Africa, Cairo is home to more than 11 million people. Many tourists come to visit the city, particularly the 4,500-year-old pyramids.

Safaa from Egypt

Ten-year-old Safaa lives in Abu Sir, a neighborhood about 20 miles (30 km) from the center of Cairo, the capital of Egypt. She is the youngest of six children—three girls and three boys. Safaa's father works on archeological digs and as a tour guide, and her mother sells goods in the local market.

School building

Safaa's school is in a specially built building with its own restrooms and a small schoolyard. The school is free to attend and all the girls consider themselves very lucky to go there because their families could not afford the costs of uniforms and travel at other schools.

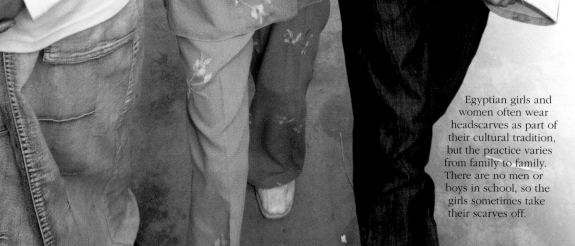

Safaa

Egyptian girls and women often wear headscarves as part of their cultural tradition, but the practice varies from family to family. There are no men or boys in school, so the girls sometimes take their scarves off.

Walking to school

It takes Safaa just 15 minutes to walk to school with her sister Yasmine and their friend Hanaa. They sometimes buy a snack on the way. The school day runs from 8 a.m. to 1 p.m., Saturday to Wednesday. The building is open some of the time during the summer vacation for girls who need to catch up on work or who want to use the library.

The schoolyard

Here, in the courtyard of the school's yard, the girls discuss a topic—urban pollution—without the teachers being present. Sometimes they also get projects to go off and research independently. This kind of active learning is very popular with the students.

All the children helped to decorate the courtyard. Safaa painted these flowers on the wall.

There are colorful signs in Arabic and English.

Everybody enjoys jumping rope.

There are no organized sports, but the girls love to run around and play on the school's yard.

Time to eat

At midmorning, classes stop so the girls can eat. Safaa eats a typical Egyptian breakfast, which consists of pitta bread, falafel (deep-fried chickpea balls), and *ful medames* (broad or fava beans).

Falafel

Ful

Pitta

The classroom

There are 36 girls in the school aged seven to 14, with a further 20 on the waiting list. They are all taught in one big classroom by their two teachers, whom they call "Miss." Girls who misbehave are made to stand apart and are not allowed to participate in the class.

Fun classroom games help develop the girls' coordination.

Safaa and her friends take part in a role-playing activity. Safaa plays the part of a son in a family that has just found out they are being given money to start a business.

The father

☀ **" My teacher is my favorite person. My greatest wish is to complete my studies and go to college to become a teacher. "**

Day-to-day

Safaa's favorite subject is Arabic and she enjoys reading stories with her classmates. She also learns English. The girls don't get homework every night but they have regular tests to make sure they are keeping up.

Tonight is a homework night. Safaa looks over her tasks with Yasmine and their father.

The country

Ethiopia is an agricultural country—it's Africa's biggest exporter of coffee—but sometimes not enough rain falls, so crops fail and people do not have enough food to eat. Less than half the population can read and write.

Semira from Ethiopia

Semira is twelve years old and lives in a children's home in Addis Ababa, the capital of Ethiopia. Some of the children at the home are orphans who lost their parents to a disease called AIDs. Semira and her friends go to a large public school that has more than 2,500 students.

Children at the home are enthusiastic readers. Here they are unloading a donation of books from the US.

Good health

The home is run by three adults and the children refer to them as their "parents." It also has its own nurse. She makes sure the children are healthy and gives them medicine when they need it. Semira is a Muslim and chooses to wear a headscarf to school. This is a Muslim sign of modesty.

Semira wants people to understand what it is like to grow up in Ethiopia. She is writing a book about her experiences.

School is 30 minutes' walk from the home. The children walk together, the older ones looking after the little ones.

Home life

There are 14 children in Semira's home and she enjoys living with so many children. She shares a dormitory with seven other girls. At night they leave the light on because the younger ones are afraid of the dark.

Semira helps to make traditional Ethiopian bread, called injera.

The home's weekly groceries include lots of fresh vegetables.

In class

Semira's school

Semira has nine different subjects, each with a different teacher. There are 70 students in her class. Semira first went to school when she was five, but some of her classmates started school later and these children are now 15 years old.

Lunchtime

Semira and her friends take sack lunches to school. Today's lunch is rice and vegetables. This was prepared by the home's cook, who makes healthy, largely vegetarian, dishes.

...I saw a program about an early human skeleton named Lucy. I'd like to be an archeologist and discover the next one.

The lessons

Semira's favorite subject is math because she thinks the teacher is very good. She also likes biology and would like to study science when she is older. Teaching is mostly done from the blackboard, since there is not enough room to work in small groups.

Susan from Botswana

Susan is nine and lives in a village in southeast Botswana. Because both of her parents have died, Susan is looked after by her grandmother. Susan goes to school in the sprawling town of Molepolole, then to an after-school program for orphans and children whose parents need help caring for them.

Susan's school
Susan's school is close to her home and it takes only a few minutes to walk there. She starts at 7:30 a.m. and finishes at 12:30 p.m. During the day the students are given a snack of bread and milk.

Although Botswana is roughly the size of the UK, fewer than two million people live there. That is about the number of people who live in a large US city.

The roof is made of straw (called thatch) held in place by ribbons. On some huts these are brightly colored.

In Susan's village, mud huts sit alongside buildings made of bricks. Cooking is usually done on a stove outside. Susan likes living with her grandmother and thinks she is very kind.

The huts have no running water so villagers have to carry buckets from the well nearby.

Susan's older brother and two sisters also live with their grandmother. One of Susan's sisters has a baby of her own.

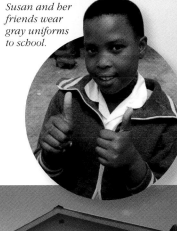

Susan and her friends wear gray uniforms to school.

Class time

There are 31 boys and girls in Susan's class. Their teacher is Miss Reetsand and Susan calls her "teacher." Miss Reetsand is Susan's hero—Susan thinks she is very beautiful.

Children take turns writing answers on the blackboard.

Written work

Susan is taught in English and the national language, Setswana. Her favorite subjects are English and math.

Susan has written in her workbook in Setswana.

This book is used by Susan in her social studies class.

After-school program

After school, Susan goes to a day-care center for orphans, where more than 400 children are looked after each day. Here she can talk freely to counselors, who help her cope with not having parents.

Susan has decorated her pencil case with a picture of the soccer player Khumo Motlhabane, who plays for the national team.

☀ ❝ . . . I hope that one day I can be a nurse and help people who are sick and make them well. ❞

Susan eats dinner at the day-care center and helps to wash up afterward.

Bible reading

At the day-care center Susan has classes in Bible studies. Teachers at the center also help Susan with her school homework, since Susan finds this difficult.

Europe

This continent stretches from the cold lands north of the Arctic Circle to the warm and sunny countries of Spain and Greece. In Europe, education in schools has been part of a tradition going back thousands of years, and Europe is home to some of the world's oldest schools and universities.

This is Europe

Denmark

The capital city of Denmark is Copenhagen. This sea-facing city is home to Queen Margrethe, from the oldest royal family in the world.

The Netherlands

Much of the Netherlands lies below sea level. Windmills were used to pump out water to keep the land from flooding. The Netherlands is the world's biggest exporter of cut flowers and bulbs.

Belgium

The Atomium monument (below) is in Brussels, Belgium's capital city. Belgium has three official languages: people speak Dutch, French, or German.

Ireland

Often called the Emerald Isle because of its green pastures, Ireland has a long tradition of music, dance, and poetry.

England

England is part of the United Kingdom, which also includes Wales, Scotland, and Northern Ireland. London is the capital and one of the biggest cities in Europe.

Poland

Krakow, Poland's former capital, is a major cultural center. It is home to Jagiellonian University, Poland's oldest and most prestigious university.

ICELAND

NORWAY

SWEDEN

FINLAND

Saint Petersburg

ESTONIA

RUSSIAN FEDERATION

DENMARK
Vejen

LATVIA

Moscow

LITHUANIA

Tullydonnell
IRELAND

UNITED KINGDOM

KALININGRAD
(RUSSIAN FEDERATION)

London

Amsterdam

NETHERLANDS

BELARUS

Brussels
BELGIUM

GERMANY

POLAND

Paris

LUXEMBOURG

FRANCE

E U R O P E

CZECH REPUBLIC

Krakow

UKRAINE

Schwabhausen

SLOVAKIA

SWITZERLAND

AUSTRIA

HUNGARY

MOLDOVA

Milan

SLOVENIA

ROMANIA

PORTUGAL

SPAIN

ANDORRA

CROATIA

SAN MARINO

ITALY

BOSNIA & HERZEGOVINA

SERBIA

Madrid

MONTENEGRO

BULGARIA

ALBANIA

MACEDONIA

Istanbul

TURKEY

GREECE

Germany

Germany has a wealth of history and landscapes, from fairy-tale castles, like Neuschwanstein (shown here), to forests and Bavarian mountains.

Spain

Spain is a vast and varied country with differing languages, cultures, and traditions that vary by region. Flamenco dancing is a southern specialty.

France

France is the most visited country in the world. The Eiffel Tower dominates the skyline in the capital city, Paris. The tower receives six million visitors each year.

Italy

Because of its shape, Italians fondly refer to their country as *lo Stivale* (the boot). It is composed of many independent states, which were only unified into one country in 1861.

Francis from England

Francis is nine years old and lives in London with his parents, two sisters, and one brother. Francis and both of his sisters go to the same school. They walk there, often meeting friends along the way.

Children wear navy pants, shorts, or skirts with the school sweatshirt. Girls can also wear a blue and white checkered dress in the summer.

Classroom

There are 30 children in Francis's class. Their teacher is Mr. Brady. Each classroom has a whiteboard, which the teacher can write on but which is also linked to a computer so it can be used to show pictures, charts, and movies.

There is a school cafeteria, but Francis brings a sack lunch. He always has some fruit.

Assembly

Each assembly has a theme. Today, Francis's grade has gathered for an assembly about St. George, the patron saint of England. They are using songbooks to sing a song about him.

A model bird, part of a project on birds.

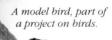

Bird project

The class is making nesting boxes. These will be hung from trees in the school grounds to attract small birds.

This is the nesting box that Francis has made.

In this activity the children are playing at being a soccer player and a TV interviewer. Francis is using a rolled-up piece of paper as a pretend microphone.

Francis is learning to play the guitar. He tries to practice every evening.

On summer evenings, when the weather is good, Francis plays cricket in his yard.

With his dad, Francis carries the recycling box to the sidewalk for pickup.

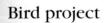

Michael from Ireland

Michael lives in Tullydonnell in County Louth, about 50 miles (80 km) north of Dublin. He goes to the local school where there are about 120 pupils. His favorite playground games are soccer and pretend wrestling.

School is only two fields away from Michael's home. Michael started coming here when he was five, although some children start when they are four or six. He has lots of friends, some from his own school, and some from other local schools whom he met when his father ran a pub.

School bus
About 50 children take the school bus. Michael likes to look out for Clonmore Castle on the journey.

Classroom
The 28 children in second and third grade share a classroom. They have two teachers. Mrs. McKeown teaches mostly in Irish, and Miss Boylan in English.

Michael likes to sit near the front of the class.

Nature lesson
The children are planting bulbs. They have been learning about different trees and plants and are also using what they have learned in their art classes.

Learning Gaelic
The children spend half their time at school learning Irish Gaelic. Michael says this is his least favorite subject, although he is very good at it.

Michael is good at soccer and spends a lot of time practicing.

The class travels to the local swimming pool once a week for swimming lessons.

Michael's classmates stand by the brightly colored mural on the playground wall.

Michael's family
Michael, who is eight years old, is the oldest of five children. His sister Roisin is six, twins Katie and Patrick are four, and Cormac is six months.

Day-to-day

At school, Anna is making a magazine of her recent school trip, when she spent 10 days in the mountains. She skied and also visited caves that had lots of limestone stalagmites and stalactites.

Anna from France

Anna is 10 years old and lives in Paris, France. Her home is a fifth-floor apartment in the center of the city. Anna's school is so close she can see it from her living room window. Each day, she goes downstairs to the street, crosses at the crosswalk, and moments later she is in class.

> **I love art, math, science, history, and gymnastics.**

Paris is the capital of France, and the center of politics, business, fashion, and the arts. It is home to the Louvre Museum and art gallery, with its distinctive glass pyramid. Some of the world's most famous pictures are kept at the Louvre.

This is the view from Anna's apartment.

Anna lives with her mother, father, and eight-year-old sister, Sophie.

The high life

Anna's parents have lived in their apartment for 20 years. Anna loves knowing all her neighbors. Each year they gather together for a party where they eat and drink and chat. Anna shares a bedroom with Sophie, but would prefer to have her own room.

School days

Anna often makes her own breakfast of cereal and orange juice. Then she walks to school with Sophie. There is no school on Wednesdays, so Anna and Sophie get up late. They play board games, or pretend to be teacher and student. They go to school every other Saturday.

Anna's favorite subject is art. This is one of her paintings.

Sometimes Anna has tests at school. She doesn't mind being tested, but she likes to get good grades.

This playground can be seen from the school building. It is for little children.

In class

There are 24 children in Anna's class. At the beginning of each school year, the stores get crowded with children buying *les fournitures scolaires*—a long list of materials they need for each of their classes, including pens, pencils, and notebooks.

Lunchtime

Children have an hour and a half for lunch, which they eat in the school cafeteria. Anna would prefer to take a sack lunch to school, but children are not usually allowed to do this in France. Anna does not always eat all her lunch.

Anna has chosen rice salad, bread, chicken, beans, pineapple, and yogurt.

Playground fun

There are three playgrounds at Anna's school. Anna and her friends like to play catch. When it is cold, they stay inside and read in the library.

Home time

Anna spends about an hour each evening on her homework. She works at a desk in her bedroom. After she finishes, she reads and plays with Sophie and their stuffed animals. These are kept in their own little house on a shelf. The animals' feet are magnetic so they can stick to a metal surface such as a fridge.

Anna has had guitar lessons for two years. These are strict and she has to pass exams each year to be able to continue.

Alvaro and Nacho from Spain

Ten-year-old twins Alvaro and Nacho live in Torrelodones, 13 miles (20 km) northwest of Madrid. Their mother drives them and their two cousins to school every day. The boys are in different classes but they both like science and dislike languages.

Many people who live in Torrelodones travel into Madrid, the capital of Spain, to work.

Alvaro

Nacho

At home
The boys live with their parents. The family has a housekeeper named Maria, but she does not live with them.

The twins eat breakfast with their father before leaving for school in the car.

The school uniform is gray pants with a navy blazer and tie.

Many children find it more comfortable to use carts rather than backpacks to carry their schoolbooks.

School building
Spanish summers can be extremely hot so the school was designed with the heat in mind. Special blinds keep the sun out while allowing the air to circulate.

The children call their teachers *Don* ("Mr.") followed by their first names. Nacho's homeroom teacher is Don José.

Art class
Each child has their own desk, but for art classes the desks are pushed together so eight or 10 children can work in a group.

Alvaro holds up his picture.

Science class
The teacher shows Nacho how to use a microscope during a science lesson. Nacho says he is interested in becoming a scientist or else a lawyer when he grows up. Alvaro would like to be a biologist or a mathematician.

Who's in class?
There are both boys and girls at the school. Alvaro's class has 22 children and Nacho's has 18. In his class Alvaro sits at the front on the left, near to the teacher. Nacho sits at the front of his class too.

Lunchtime
The children eat lunch at around noon. Each class takes turns eating in the school cafeteria. The school kitchen prepares fresh, healthy food every day.

Lunch is paella and an omelette with melon for dessert.

Nacho takes part in a relay race.

Sports
The boys go to soccer practice after school on Mondays and Wednesdays, and there's usually a game on Saturdays. In the playground during recess they also play soccer, as well as basketball, and *pilla-pilla* (catch) with their friends.

The boys have a soccer ball signed by the Real Madrid team.

The boys are learning to play the recorder and the guitar at school.

> ❝...I would like to be a professional trial bike rider. You ride near rivers and rocks and in forests. You have to be very skilled. ❞

Homework
The school week runs from 9:20 a.m. to 4:30 p.m. Monday to Friday. The boys do about two hours of homework every night. They have tests twice a week on Wednesdays and Fridays—once a month in English, and three times a month in science, math, and Spanish.

Day-to-day
Everyone at school is expected to dress neatly. Both teachers and pupils wear shirts and ties. If a child misbehaves at school they have to stay in at recess and a letter is sent to their parents.

Both boys have trial bikes, which they ride off-road in the countryside. In trial biking, riders have to navigate a very difficult course full of obstacles without allowing their feet to touch the ground.

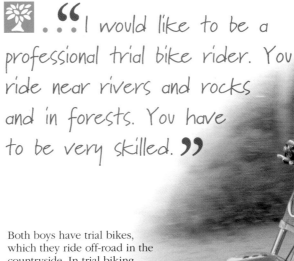

Flora from Belgium

Flora is eight years old and lives in Brussels, the capital of Belgium. She has an older brother named Raphael. They both go to an international school and their friends' families come from all over the world.

🌳 **"**...I like my school a lot. It's special. But my favorite place is the playground.**"**

Coline has one white paw.

Flora loves everything about animals. She has a pet rabbit named Coline, who runs fast and sometimes bites.

Marketplace
Brussels has two official languages, French and Dutch, and all street signs are written in both languages. It is a market city selling everything from birds and horses to flowers and food.

This horse is one of Flora's favorite toys. She hopes to have a real horse one day.

Flora and Raphael travel to school by bus. The bus stops at the end of their road at 7:30 a.m., and in winter it is still dark at that time. They take all the books they need for the day, carrying them in heavy bags.

Each day a child reads a thought for the day aloud and the children discuss it. Today's thought is: "Good design is making objects as beautiful as they are useful."

School for all
There are about 3,000 pupils in Flora's school aged from five to 18. Both boys and girls are in her class. Children wear what they like to school and they dress casually.

Working together
The children sometimes work in pairs. Here they are finding seven definitions from the dictionary. They have to use more than one dictionary to find the meanings of the more difficult words.

The children are making a timeline. It will show Earth's history from the first animals to the present day.

Tintin comes to school
Cartoon strips of Tintin and his faithful dog, Snowy, were drawn by a man called Hergé, who lived in Brussels. Scenes from the *Tintin* books decorate the entrance hall of the school.

Lunchtime
Students can choose either a vegetarian or a meat dish each day. It is put on their table and they serve themselves. Flora likes meat and vegetables, but she doesn't like fish.

Flora loves music and is learning the piano. She has been playing for six months.

Every evening Flora's parents help her to do at least one hour's homework.

> "I'd like to be a television host when I grow up."

Isabelle from the Netherlands

Isabelle is 11 years old and lives in Amsterdam, in the Netherlands. Her apartment is close to the city-center stores and museums. Each day she rides her bike to school along cycle paths that crisscross the city.

Amsterdam is built on land that used to be part of the sea. Engineers built a network of canals that are still used today to transport goods and drain rainwater from the marshy land.

Isabelle has a computer game console. She plays Sims Pets *on it.*

Family life

Isabelle lives with her mom and dad in a two-bedroom apartment. Her mom works in a bank and her dad teaches Indonesian martial arts.

Isabelle's school

Isabelle's school is made up of three buildings that sit alongside canals. They are joined together by a playground. Isabelle's classroom is on the first floor.

Isabelle has a spelling and grammar test, then she works on fractions in a math class. When the children have finished their work, they make themselves a cup of tea in the classroom if they want to.

Isabelle's teacher, Franz, is an enthusiastic musician who plays the guitar to his class. Isabelle and many of her friends are learning to play the guitar, too.

The art class

The children paint self-portraits, copying the style of the artist Picasso. They mix their colors in old egg cartons, which can be recycled afterward.

Isabelle has painted herself from three different angles.

This is the Spanish artist, Pablo Picasso.

Isabelle's school does not have a kitchen. The children bring in food from home.

In bad weather the children stay inside and play games such as football.

Most days Isabelle and her friends like to play basketball and soccer.

After school Isabelle goes to martial arts class with her dad.

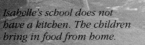

Søren from Denmark

Søren goes to school in Vejen, a small town in Denmark. He is 10 years old and an avid soccer player. He was named Søren after a famous soccer player, Søren Lerby, who played for Bayern Munich and for Denmark.

Miniature Danish flags stand in the corner of Søren's classroom.

There are about 500 boys and girls at Søren's school, aged 10 to 14 years.

Cycling to school.

Getting around

Cycling makes Søren very independent. He travels to school along peaceful bike paths, but there is one busy road he has to cross by himself. Søren has traveled all over Denmark to play in soccer matches with the local youth team. He hopes to become a professional soccer player one day.

Colorful carnival masks made by Søren and his classmates

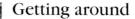

In the library

There are a few computers in the school library, but not enough for every child so they have to take turns.

Learning

Søren's class studies English, history, and math, with a different teacher for each subject. They get about half an hour's homework each night. Søren is currently doing a project about Einstein, which involves many experiments.

The children play "Simon Says" in their English lesson. The length of the school day varies but usually runs from 8 a.m. to 1 p.m.. There is no school uniform and the children call the teachers by their first names.

The children gobble down their lunch quickly so they can go and play soccer for the rest of the lunch break. The girls play, too.

Family life

Søren has a younger brother of eight, and two sisters of 12 and 14. The oldest is away at boarding school. When he is 14, Søren hopes to go to a boarding school that specializes in soccer.

Søren has been playing the guitar for five years, and the piano for two.

The family adopted two stray cats.

Søren enjoys computer games.

" I once went by myself to Copenhagen on the train. I played computer games. It was fine. "

A bright mural decorates a school corridor. Ciao means hello.

Chiara from Italy

Eleven-year-old Chiara has recently started middle school. She lives in a town near Milan, Italy, and has two older brothers—one goes to a different school and the other has left school.

Rolling hills

Chiara's hometown, Villa d'Adda, is about 22 miles (35 km) northeast of Milan, in the foothills of the Alps. The town is famous in Italy for its ferry, which is based on a drawing by Leonardo da Vinci.

A former monastery

The spacious school building, set in large grounds, has its own lake. It used to be a monastery. There are 28 children in Chiara's class—14 girls and 14 boys, all aged 10 or 11. At the moment they are revising material they learned in primary school.

Chiara's class visits the school's chapel, which is very grand. The children are still getting to know each other and learning to find their way around the school and its grounds.

Chiara loves bright colors.

Chiara only recently moved to this school. The children each sit at their own desk, with the desks usually arranged in a horseshoe shape.

The whole class is learning to play the recorder. Chiara's favorite subject is Italian literature.

Chiara spends more than three hours a day on her homework.

> **❝...I help Mom to clean the house and empty the dishwasher. I'm good because I listen to my mom.❞**

Chiara's favorite toy is a tiny dog, which is only 2 in (5 cm) long.

Every Monday Chiara visits her grandparents for a lunch of home-cooked spaghetti and meatballs.

Family ties

Chiara's mother is a teacher and her father is a writer and journalist. Chiara's grandparents live nearby. She likes to go walking with them and their dog.

Chiara can ride a horse. She is learning to jump, starting with low poles and then building up.

She also enjoys playing on her swing, riding her bike, skateboarding, and taking country walks.

Fanny from Germany

Fanny is nine years old and lives with her parents, brother, and baby sister on the edge of a small village in southern Germany. Her school is 2 miles (3.5 km) away in a nearby town, and she travels there by bus.

Country setting
Fanny's village sits in flat farmland surrounded by small, rolling hills. Many of the roads have separate cycle paths.

Fanny likes reading books that are full of pictures.

This pony's legs bend forward so it can lie down.

Brother and sister
Fanny's brother, Felix, is seven years old and goes to school with Fanny. Their little sister, Lilly, is eight months old. Fanny thinks Lilly is sweet and likes to carry her around and read to her. When Lilly cries at night she wakes Fanny up.

Bus to school
Each morning the bus picks up about 50 children and takes them to their school in Schwabhausen. Fanny's bus stop is across the road from her house. The bus drops the children outside school in time for an 8 a.m. start.

Classes last for 45 minutes. School finishes at 1 p.m., when the children go home for lunch.

Day-to-day
Fanny goes to school from Mondays to Fridays. Each day she has an hour of homework, which she does in her bedroom. Normally she does it right after lunch, so that it is out of the way and she can play.

Modern building
The school building is about 15 years old. Solar panels on the roof generate electricity to heat the classrooms. Inside it is light and bright, with children's colorful artwork decorating the walls. There are 24 children in Fanny's class, aged eight or nine. Fanny is the oldest.

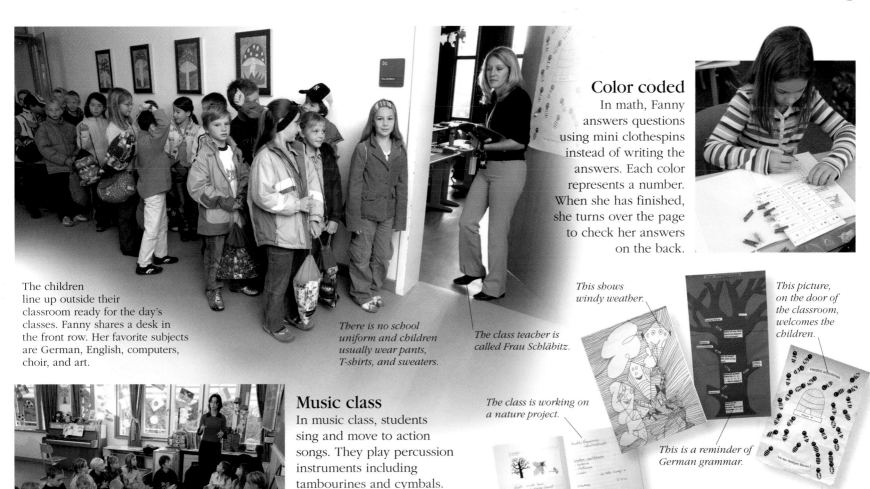

The children line up outside their classroom ready for the day's classes. Fanny shares a desk in the front row. Her favorite subjects are German, English, computers, choir, and art.

There is no school uniform and children usually wear pants, T-shirts, and sweaters.

The class teacher is called Frau Schläbitz.

Color coded

In math, Fanny answers questions using mini clothespins instead of writing the answers. Each color represents a number. When she has finished, she turns over the page to check her answers on the back.

This shows windy weather.

This picture, on the door of the classroom, welcomes the children.

The class is working on a nature project.

This is a reminder of German grammar.

Students draw and color in pictures when they learn about a subject.

Music class

In music class, students sing and move to action songs. They play percussion instruments including tambourines and cymbals. Then they rehearse a musical they are performing at the end of term. Fanny loves to sing and is in the choir.

In the gym

The children play a game of cat and mouse around a huge circular sheet. Then they split into groups in different activity areas. The groups spend five minutes on one activity before moving to the next.

Fanny swirls a long ribbon. She makes big circles and figure eights.

Wobble boards are good for balance. There is a mat to land on if anyone falls.

Fanny holds on to a rope to help her climb a bench to the wall bars.

After school, Fanny and Felix play soccer on the grass behind their house.

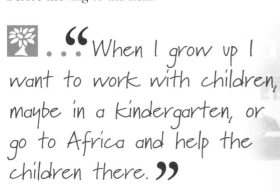

…"When I grow up I want to work with children, maybe in a kindergarten, or go to Africa and help the children there."

Day-to-day
Marek's school day runs from 8:50 a.m. until 2 p.m., but he stays for the after-school program. A teacher looks after the children. They do homework, play, read, and watch movies while their parents are at work. Marek gets home at 5 p.m.

Marek from Poland

Marek, who is eight years old is from the center of Krakow, one of Poland's major cities. He lives with his mother and father, and two cats named Szarak and Tunczyk, who sleep on Marek's bed at night. In the summer, the family visits Marek's grandmother in the countryside.

Going to school

Marek's walk to school takes him though the city along cobbled streets and through tree-lined parks. In the fall the walk takes longer because Marek likes to collect leaves and chestnuts. Krakow is famous for the pigeons in the Market Square. Marek, like most Polish children, loves to stop and feed them.

Obwarzanki *(bread rings) are a popular snack in the streets of Krakow.*

... "I like walking through the leaves."

The school was founded in 1871 and has been located in the same building since 1877.

School day

Marek is in the second grade, where most of the classes are taught by the same teacher. From the fourth grade, different subjects are taught by different teachers. Marek eats both lunch and dinner at school. After school he sometimes goes to dancing lessons. Once a week, he goes to Boy Scouts.

Work and play

Marek's best friends are Romek and Kacper. Today the children are learning about the different jobs that people do. In the school library, the librarian tells them about her work. The children also visit the school secretary and the school cook.

Marek's class visits the park near the school. They play team games, passing a ring from person to person.

They collect fallen leaves and make pictures with them on the ground.

The children are making pictures inspired by the shapes and colors of fall.

First, each child draws a flower shape by tracing around a template.

Then they cut out flower shapes, first in yellow and then again in orange paper.

Next, they cut out the leaves and stalks, this time using bright green paper.

Celebrating fall

Every semester the school chooses a topic and the children learn about it. Last year it was Polish history, and this year it's ecology. The children are learning about the seasons and animals. Next semester they will visit an organic farm.

Last, they glue the pieces to construction paper, decorating the center of the flowers with scrunched up balls of tissue paper. Then each child signs his or her picture.

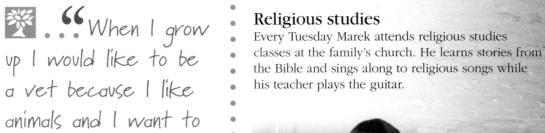

" ...When I grow up I would like to be a vet because I like animals and I want to help them. "

Marek prepares food for the cats.

Religious studies

Every Tuesday Marek attends religious studies classes at the family's church. He learns stories from the Bible and sings along to religious songs while his teacher plays the guitar.

Singing is an enjoyable way to learn.

This album is full of friendly messages from Marek's classmates.

Asia

This is the largest of all the continents, with hugely varied landscapes and climates. Schools in China have existed for 3,000 years, India has one of the oldest school systems in the world, and Japanese children have been learning their characters since 500 BCE. So it's off to school!

This is Asia

Turkey
Turkey borders eight countries, two seas, and bridges two continents— Asia and Europe. It therefore has a unique blend of Western and Eastern traditions and cultures.

The Russian Federation
The Russian Federation, the largest country in the world, spans Asia and Europe. Moscow is the capital city. At its center stands St. Basil's cathedral with its traditional Russian "onion" domes.

Mongolia
Mongolia is a land of rugged mountains, vast deserts, and dry, grassy plains called steppes. Here, wandering tribes of nomads ride horses to herd livestock including camels, cattle, and goats.

Jordan
The ancient ruins of Petra are part of Jordan's long history. Some buildings in this unique city were carved into sheer rock and date back to Roman times.

Israel
Lying at the junction of three continents— Africa, Asia, and Europe—this small country is home to Jerusalem (above), a city holy to Judaism, Christianity, and Islam.

India
India has a population of one billion—that's three times the population of the US. The country is mainly farmland, and in the north is the biggest mountain range in the world, the Himalayas.

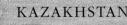

China
China has the biggest population in the world— 1.3 billion people. It boasts the world's longest structure, the Great Wall of China (below).

Japan
Zoom! Superexpress trains speed across the earthquake zones of Japan in high-tech splendor.

South Korea
One half of South Korea's population lives in or near Seoul, the buzzing capital city and one of the biggest cities in the world.

East Timor
In 2002 East Timor became the first new country of the 21st century, after gaining independence from Indonesia. This small country, with one million people, has two official languages—Portuguese and Tetum.

Map labels

Saint Petersburg
Panayevsk
RUSSIAN FEDERATION
Moscow
Istanbul
TURKEY
GEORGIA
CYPRUS
ARMENIA
AZERBAIJAN
LEBANON
SYRIA
ISRAEL
Amman
JORDAN
IRAQ
KAZAKHSTAN
UZBEKISTAN
TURKMENISTAN
KYRGYSTAN
TAJIKISTAN
ASIA
MONGOLIA
Kharkorin
NORTH KOREA
Seoul
SOUTH KOREA
JAPAN
Chiba
IRAN
AFGHANISTAN
CHINA
Shanghai
KUWAIT
BAHRAIN
QATAR
U.A.E.
SAUDI ARABIA
PAKISTAN
Delhi
Mussoorie
NEPAL
BHUTAN
BANGLADESH
TAIWAN
OMAN
YEMEN
INDIA
MYANMAR (BURMA)
LAOS
VIETNAM
THAILAND
CAMBODIA
PHILIPPINES
SRI LANKA
BRUNEI
MALAYSIA
SINGAPORE
INDONESIA
Maliana
EAST TIMOR

Ksenia from the Russian Federation

Ksenia is 12 and lives in St. Petersburg, in the Russian Federation. She goes to an Academy school. Here more subjects are taught than in other public schools, including folklore, journalism, and languages.

St. Petersburg was founded 300 years ago. It has grand buildings and canals and was once home to the ruling families of Russia.

... "When I grow up I'd like to work with people. Maybe I'll be a translator."

The school
Ksenia's school used to be a church. It doesn't have sports fields, but Ksenia doesn't mind since it has an indoor gym. The school hires security guards to check who comes into the building. They are paid for by parents.

Where to sit
Children mostly sit where they choose. Sometimes though, the teacher makes girls sit next to boys to stop children from chatting. Ksenia doesn't think this works.

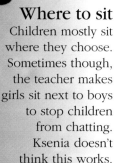

Ksenia's painting of trees

Working away
Ksenia has art classes at school as well as at the Hermitage Museum nearby. In the summer, the class stays at a monastery off the coast of St. Petersburg where they learn about the natural surroundings.

Olga from the Russian Federation

Olga is eight years
old and goes to school in Moscow, in the Russian Federation. Olga is unable to walk and has to use a wheelchair. She goes to a regular school with nearly 400 other children from the city. Ramps have been built in the school so that Olga can travel around with ease.

Olga works hard in class and enjoys drawing and finding out about the stars and planets. At home she likes to watch the Russian cartoon character Cheburashka, a fairy tale animal from a tropical rain forest. She would make her own real-life Cheburashka, if she could.

Alexei from the Russian Federation

Alexei is 10 years old and lives near Panayevsk, in the icy north of the Russian Federation. Alexei comes from reindeer-herding people called Nenets. Each year he spends three months with his family, then, as winter draws near, he travels to boarding school in a helicopter. He lives there for the next nine months.

Children look out of a helicopter window

Taking flight
Children like Alexei first go off to boarding school when they are about seven. Helicopters are also used to deliver supplies and mail. They can fly in temperatures below freezing—only heavy snow or strong winds stop them.

Cold walk
Since school is made up of several separate buildings, children have to walk across the frozen playground to go from one to another. They play outside in all but the most severe weather.

Today lunch is steaming hot soup. Favorite foods include reindeer meat and fish.

Lassos are used to catch hold of reindeer. Alexei has one made from nylon.

A school day
Alexei has classes on weekdays and Saturday mornings. He speaks Russian and the reindeer herders' language, Nenets. Nenets has many words to describe snow, reindeer breeding, hunting, and fishing.

Children go to bed at 9 p.m. and rise at 7 a.m. Usually 2–8 children share a room, sleeping under thick comforters.

" ...My friends are important to me. We do our homework all together at my house. **"**

Aysima from Turkey

Aysima is 11 years old and lives with her family in Istanbul, Turkey. Her school overlooks the Bosphorus, a strip of water that flows through the city and separates Asia and Europe.

Aysima lives with her mother, father, and younger sister.

Breakfast

On school days Aysima eats cereal and fruit for breakfast. On weekends she has a breakfast of tomatoes, white cheese, olives, bread, and honey. This is washed down with strong black tea, called *çay*, diluted with hot water.

Tea

Hot water

This is a Turkish mosque.

In the evenings, Aysima packs her school bag with a textbook and workbook for each class the next day.

This is an Armenian church.

On the streets

Aysima travels to school by car or on the school bus. She doesn't like the busy rush-hour traffic because it holds her up and often makes her late for school.

Day-to-day

During the week, Aysima studies her favorite subjects, Turkish and English. When a child misbehaves, the whole class is punished. They might have to write out the same sentence 10 times—neatly!

Aysima lives in a multicultural area of Istanbul where mosques, churches, and synagogues are built close together. Both Armenian and Turkish children go to Aysima's school and both languages are spoken there.

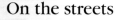

Aysima at school

Aysima moved to her school a year ago. She already has lots of friends who visit her at home. Now that she is 11 she wears a gray and pink uniform. Up to the age of 10, the uniform is blue.

Old school

There are 34 students in Aysima's class. She feels very lucky because some schools in Turkey have up to 70 children in a class. Aysima's school building once belonged to Marko Pasha, a court official who lived around 150 years ago. He listened to people's complaints, and even today there is a saying in Turkey, "Go tell your problem to Marko Pasha." On weekends, the popular TV program *Hayat Bilgisi* (Life Knowledge) is filmed at the school.

Homework

Aysima lives high up in an apartment block. When the weather is good she does her homework on the balcony. There she can hear the mosques in the area making the call to prayer. She likes working on projects best, particularly ones on the Aegean region of Turkey and Greece.

Aysima made a frame for this picture of Istanbul.

This page shows historical buildings and monuments.

After school

Aysima's father is a volleyball instructor and Aysima likes to play volleyball after school. She is also planning to take a course in Turkish folk dancing. Every region has its own dances, with particular costumes, steps, and instruments.

This dance for the bride represents love, marriage, and the night before the wedding.

Some dances are only performed by women and girls.

This is a bracelet.

These beaded slippers are not made to be worn.

Beads are threaded onto a metal frame.

Make it

Aysima loves to cook and often prepares food for her friends to eat. She also spends hours making things with beads, including jewelry, candle holders, and colorful slippers.

Ramadan

During the month of Ramadan, adult Muslims traditionally fast (do not eat) from dawn until dusk. Aysima goes to the baker to buy *iftar* bread, which she will share with her parents when they break their fast in the evening.

Dana from Jordan

Dana is 10 years old and lives in Amman, the capital of Jordan. She has an eight-year-old brother called Karam. The pair travel to their school by bus. The trip takes about 30 minutes.

Dana with her cousin Rania, who is in the same class.

School campus

Dana's school has a running track and a full-size, 400-seat theater, which is also used by the local community. There are science laboratories and computer rooms as well. Dana's favorite subject is English. About 1,000 pupils attend her school.

Mixed classes

Many pupils are Jordanian, but some come from elsewhere in the Middle East, Africa, and Europe. Lessons are in English and Arabic—most of the children are bilingual.

Special project

Dana's class is learning about the solar system. The students have made a model of the planets and their orbits around the Sun.

Dana plays with her friends before school starts at 8 a.m. Classes end at 2:30 p.m.

"...I want to be a designer or a famous actress when I leave school."

Dana with her parents and younger brother Karam.

Dana is an avid dancer. She takes ballet lessons twice a week and has been learning since she was four years old.

At home after school, Dana roller skates while Rania rides beside her on a scooter.

Salam is Arabic for "peace."

Yotam from Israel

Eleven-year-old Yotam lives in a village midway between Jerusalem and Tel Aviv. Although Jewish and Arab people have fought over religion and territory in his country, Yotam goes to a mixed school where children study together in harmony.

In the classroom

There are 26 children in Yotam's class, all aged 11 or 12. There are about the same number of girls and boys. The children don't wear a uniform, and they call their teachers by their first names. The children have language classes in Hebrew, Arabic, and English. There are exams once a semester.

Yotam looks forward to recess, as he likes to run around with the other children.

The school promotes peace and friendship between Jewish and Arab people. A rainbow gate marks the entry to the playground.

Yotam is Jewish, while his friend Amir is a Palestinian Arab.

Special studies

Yotam's favorite classes are music and sports. He is learning to play the recorder and the guitar. He also enjoys learning about medieval history and collects historical figures.

Yotam likes working on his computer. He is currently designing a website.

He has about one hour of homework each night.

Deepak from India

Deepak is eight years old and lives with his mother, father, and 10-year-old brother, Atul, in Mussoorie in the foothills of the Himalaya mountains in India. Deepak wants to do well in school and works hard. Each day he spends five hours there, then goes home and studies for another two to three hours. He hopes to become a scientist one day and discover a new planet.

Day-to-day

Deepak goes to school every day without fail even when he doesn't feel like it. He only misses school when he is sick. Sometimes he is taken on a picnic to the fields near his school.

Deepak

Atul

Deepak's family

Deepak lives on a rabbit farm where his father works as the groundskeeper. Deepak's elder brother was born in the neighboring country of Nepal. Then the family moved to India and Deepak was born. Deepak speaks Hindi and Nepali at home and English at school.

For lunch Deepak takes flat, pan-fried bread called paratha with jam or pickles. Both his parents cook.

Deepak carries his lunch in metal pans that stack together. Metal clasps hold the lid on, and the handle folds down flat.

Deepak loves playing outdoors—climbing walls, cycling, and playing badminton. At home, he likes watching TV and playing with his favorite toy car.

Foot work

It takes Deepak, Atul, and their mother half an hour to walk to school each day. The boys have a bicycle, which they share, but they don't ride it to school. They go together with their mother, who is a helper at their school. She rings the bell at the end of classes.

Wild animals, including deer, wild boar, and leopards, live in the rocky hillside where Deepak goes to school. Deepak's mother has even seen a leopard in the trees near their house. Leopards usually leave people alone, but during hard winters they may attack farm animals.

A leopard's spotted coat acts as camouflage.

High learning

Deepak's school is built from wood, stone, and brick, and sits high up on the hillside. Inside the building, the classrooms are arranged in a row with no corridor, so he has to walk through lots of other classrooms to reach his own. Deepak's favorite subject is English. He also enjoys making things in art classes.

Mahatma Gandhi, politician and spiritual leader, believed in nonviolence to achieve swaraj—self-rule for India.

" ...I like Gandhi, who is called Bapu (Father). He helped us get freedom from the British. "

Good citizens

Each morning the children line up to sing the national anthem before they file into class. One of Deepak's favorite classes is moral science, where he learns how to help people in need. He is glad that children from any religion are allowed to study at his school. If students misbehave, they have to stand on a bench and hold up their hands.

Deepak enjoys drawing, and got an A+ grade in art. Here he has drawn a diagram to show how water moves around a house.

Water moves downward because of the force of gravity.

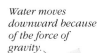

In the playground, Deepak drinks water overflowing from a tank that is filled from mountain springs.

" ...I wish for very good grades on my exams. "

Question time

Deepak has exams four times a year and short tests all year round. During morning assembly, students read the day's newspapers and answer questions on current events and general knowledge. They call their teacher "ma'am."

Water is collected from melting snow on the hilltops. It runs into pipes and down to farms and houses. Any unused water trickles out of the pipes to feed the vegetation.

There are 19 children in Deepak's class, including five girls. Deepak likes girls, although most of his friends are boys.

Sumandhara from India

Sumandhara is eight years old and lives with her parents and older sister in Delhi, the capital and second largest city of India. In her school, Sumandhara is taught in Hindi, the official language of the country.

"I like environmental studies a lot. We did a project on how we can reduce air pollution. We should plant more trees."

School building
Sumandhara's school has gardens and sports grounds, a big hall, and science, math, and computer labs. Every class has a "home period," when children are free to draw, read, or play. Sudmandhara likes her teacher very much and calls her "Usha Aunty."

Sumandhara's ID badge shows her name, her class, and who to call if she is hurt or ill.

Sumandhara likes drawing. She prefers it to studying.

Sumandhara wears a school uniform—girls can chose between pants and skirts. Sumandhara likes the nursery class best because the children there can wear any clothes they like.

These are Sumandhara's crayons. She also has colored pencils. Her favorite color is pink.

Abhinandan
Children and teachers greet everybody by waving their hands. They call it *abhinandan*. They also wave to say "thank you" and to applaud. It is their way of reducing noise at school.

Sumandhara plays with her friends on the bus to school.

The children share desks and change places on Tuesdays.

Students use building blocks to solve math problems.

Children love to play during lunch break and games period.

Reena from India

Reena is eight years old and lives in Noida, a satellite town of Delhi, in northern India. Reena stays at home during the day to look after her younger sister, Santoshi. She goes to school at night.

This is the entrance to Reena's night school.

❝...❝My parents are planning to enroll me in a day school but I don't know when they will be able to do it. I don't mind staying at home.❞

Reena practises her numbers on the blackboard. This is made from a kind of flexible plastic that can be rolled and stored in a corner.

A school night
Reena goes to school from 7:30 p.m. until 9 p.m. Boys go there from 9 p.m. onward. Reena is learning the alphabet. She knows how to add, but cannot subtract yet.

Family life
Reena lives with her family in a one-room brick house. Her father paints houses and her mother works as a stone mason at construciton sites. Reena has one brother and four sisters. Her eldest sister is married.

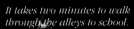
It takes two minutes to walk through the alleys to school.

There are no desks or chairs, but the carpet is soft and dry.

Volunteers teach everyone from toddlers to adults.

Reena enjoys night school as she loves to learn new things.

Xinpei from China

Xinpei is six years old and lives in southwest China. Her parents are farmers, and in the countryside where Xinpei lives, school is often a long way from a child's home. However, a new school has been built 3 miles (5 km) from Xinpei's house, so she goes to school there.

Most couples in China are only allowed to have one child to stop the country's population from growing too fast. Because Xinpei's parents live in the countryside, they could have a second child. He is named Xinwang.

Trip to school
Xinpei walks to school with friends from her village. On the way they play and pick flowers. They cross a flood wall that stops the river from damaging farmland during the rainy season. It takes an hour and a half to get to school.

This hula-hoop belongs to the school. Xinpei dreams that one day she will own one herself.

Catching a ride
During bad weather, parents drive all the local children to school. They operate a relay system, taking one group of children, then going back for the next.

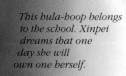

Day-to-day
Xinpei arrives at school early and plays hula-hoop with her friends before class starts at 8 a.m. The children have to clean up their classrooms and sweep the floor before they go home at 3:30 p.m.

A school day
Each Monday the whole school stands at attention while the national anthem is played over a loudspeaker and the national flag is hoisted up the flagpole. The principal makes a speech.

"...Going to school was a dream I never thought would come true, but then they opened the new school in my village. I am happy to go to school."

Two to a desk

Children sit in pairs and keep their books inside their desks. They study things like Chinese, math, and music. Although going to school is free, parents are usually expected to pay for essentials such as books and pencils. These can be too expensive for poor families, so some children are not sent to school. However, in Xinpei's school, these things are free.

This picture by Xinpei is called In spring and fall time. *The ducks live on the pond by Xinpei's house.*

It's eye time

Every day the class performs 10 minutes of eye exercises to music. These are designed to relax the eyes and protect eyesight. The children look up and down and side to side. Then they gently massage around their eyes, stimulating special places called acupressure points, which are important in Chinese medicine.

Time to eat

There is no cafeteria in the school, so children take sack lunches of cold rice and vegetables. They can eat these in the classrooms if it rains. One day Xinpei forgot to take her lunch to school so two of her friends shared their food with her.

Homework

After school, children pick tea. They work quickly, their small hands easily plucking the newest and tiniest leaves. In one hour a child can earn enough to buy a candy bar.

The whole school exercises in the playground each day. The school has a new uniform, but children only wear it on special occasions. Children wear red scarves if they are members of the political Communist Youth League.

In music class the teacher plays the tune *Frère Jacques* on the piano. The children sing words from a popular rhyme: "Two tigers, two tigers, running fast, running fast, one has no eyes, one has no tail, it's very strange, it's very strange."

Yiting from China

Ten-year-old Yiting and her mother leave their home in Shanghai at 7 a.m. for the short walk to school, past a playground and a toy store. Yiting has no brothers or sisters, but she usually plays with a friend after school.

My class
Yiting's class has 23 girls and seven boys. There are 750 children aged seven to 11 at the school.

The school building is about a hundred years old and very distinctive.

Hard at work
The school day lasts from 7:15 a.m. to 4:15 p.m., five days a week. Yiting calls her teacher "Zhang *Laoshi*" (Teacher Zhang). She sits at the back of the class because she is very tall.

School clothes
Most of the time the children wear their own clothes, but on Mondays they wear uniforms for the national flag raising ceremony.

Yiting's class rehearses for a dance performance in a couple of weeks' time.

Yiting demonstrates a chess move at the front of the class.

Chess lessons
Chess is often taught as an after-school activity at schools in China, but Yiting's school is particularly well-known for its pupils' achievements in chess competitions. The children have a chess class once a week for 45 minutes.

Yiting and her classmates coax their hoops along with sticks at recess.

Bouncing on a jumping board is also a favorite playground activity at Yiting's school.

Yiting's favorite class is physical education, and she also loves playing outside.

Jiyu from China

Jiyu is nine years old. He lives in Zhu Jia Jiao, a town about 30 miles (50 km) west of Shanghai, and walks to school. There are 40 children in each class and Jiyu shares a desk with his best friend. When he grows up he would like to be the best teacher in town.

Jiyu has a 20 minute walk to school.

Eye exercises

Twice a day, during the morning and afternoon breaks, the children perform a series of eye exercises. While listening to soft music, they are guided through four different moves that help their eyes to relax.

After school the children stay for a session of paper cutting, an ancient Chinese art form.

Paper cutting requires patience and care.

Children record their activities on a board.

Uniform

All the children wear the school uniform of a tracksuit. The boys' tracksuit is navy blue, while the girls' is red. The red scarf represents the Chinese flag.

Jiyu plays ti jian zi, a Chinese shuttlecock game a little like badminton, but played without a racket.

Jiyu is learning to play the erhu, a traditional Chinese musical instrument.

Hassa from Mongolia

Hassa is 10 years old and lives in Kharkorin in Mongolia. His mother died when he was born, so during the week he lives with his older sister, and on the weekends his grandmother takes care of him. Hassa goes to two different schools—a modern school and a monastery school where he is training to be a Buddhist monk.

At the monastery, Hassa wears a long loose gown called a del. *It is held in place with a sash.*

Home life
Hassa and his 18-year-old sister live in a traditional tent called a *ger*. It has a wooden frame covered with two layers of thick felt fabric, which also covers the floor. Most of Hassa's family members are nomadic herders, which means they move around to find fresh pastures for their animals.

Home cooking
Hassa's sister cooks on a stove in the middle of the ger. Smoke from the stove escapes through a hole in the roof.

Hassa likes watching films at home. His favorite movie is Shrek *and his favorite toy is this Shrek model.*

The school
Many children from nomadic herding families go to boarding schools, but because Hassa lives with his sister during the school year, he goes to a day school. The school has two sessions, one in the mornings and one in the afternoons. Hassa goes in the afternoons, from 2 p.m. until 6 p.m. There is no running water at Hassa's school, so children have to use an outside bathroom and clean their hands on antiseptic wipes.

...I will go full-time to the monastery school when I am 13. Then I'll become a Buddhist monk.

Good student

Hassa likes school and keeps up with his homework. In Mongolia, most children start school at eight years old. Hassa started when he was nine, after a year at the monastery. He is a year older than his classmates.

Hassa's class teacher serves the children

Time to eat

Hassa takes a bread roll for lunch. The school provides a drink made from raisins, which Hassa sips from a bowl.

Hassa speaks Mongolian, which is written left to right using the 33 letters of the Cyrillic alphabet.

In the classroom

There are more girls than boys in Hassa's class because some of the boys are at home helping their fathers look after the animals. The girls are at school so they can be educated, get good jobs, and take their wages home to their families. Most of the children wear school uniforms, and girls decorate their hair with pink net bows.

After school

On weekends and during school vacation, Hassa stays in the country *ger* belonging to his grandmother. Hassa helps look after the family's 400 sheep, oxen, and horses. Four times a year, Hassa helps take down the *ger* and move it to fresh grazing land.

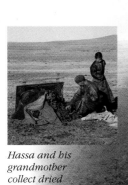

Hassa and his grandmother collect dried animal dung to burn on the fire

On weekends, Hassa goes to the monastery where he trains to be a Buddhist monk, called a lama.

The lamas *sit at low desks as they study nature and the Tibetan language. They also chant prayers.*

As well as being ridden, horses provide meat. The mares' milk is fermented to make an alcoholic drink called *airag*.

Sun-Woo from South Korea

Six-year-old Sun-Woo comes from Seoul, the capital of South Korea, where she lives with her parents and younger sister. There are over 5,000 elementary schools in South Korea where children wear their own clothes. However, Sun-Woo goes to a private school and wears a uniform.

South Korea is a mountainous and hilly nation tucked between China and Japan. Most people in South Korea live in a city—10 million in Seoul.

City lights

Sun-Woo and her family live in a modern apartment overlooking Seoul. Here, she stands at their big picture window with the lights of the city glittering behind her.

Traditionally, Korean people eat rice, fish, and *kimchi* (fermented vegetables) for breakfast, but many modern families choose Western foods instead.

School run

Sun-Woo's school is close to her home, but it takes 20 minutes to drive there in the city's heavy traffic. In the mornings, her father drops her off on the way to the furniture store he owns.

At school

Sun-Woo likes all her subjects, but English is her favorite. Each week she goes to the school forum (an open meeting), where children decide on one positive activity. Once they all agreed to be extra polite to their teachers.

Textbooks are labeled with the name of the child they belong to.

White shoes are part of Sun-Woo's uniform. When she gets to school, she takes them off, puts them in a cubby hole, and goes to class wearing slippers.

Sun-Woo's school notebook

The children form an orderly line to walk between classrooms.

... *"My heroes are my parents. My greatest wish is for my family to be happy."*

This is one of Sun-Woo's paintings.

A plant project for science class

A place to learn

There are 30 pupils in Sun-Woo's class—16 boys and 14 girls. The teacher is called Chae Mi-Jung. Sun-Woo, who is not very tall, sits at the front so she can see.

In Sun-Woo's school, there is a special classroom where the computers are kept.

Sun-Woo's finished hat is covered with brightly colored ribbons and shapes.

Making music

Sometimes in their music class Sun-Woo and her friends learn how to play a traditional Korean drum called a *jangu*, which looks like an hourglass lying on its side.

Fans are an important part of Korean costume. Like antique fans, Sun-Woo's are adorned with flowers.

Sun-Woo works hard to make one of the small, black, highly decorated hats that form part of Korean national dress.

The traditional Korean costume is called the *hanbok*. Very similar for men and women, it consists of a long, simple skirt or pants, and a short jacket. Today, the *hanbok* is worn only for special celebrations. Sun-Woo's teacher helps the children in her class to learn about Korean history, culture, and traditions like this one.

Time to eat

All the children at Sun-Woo's school have lunch in the canteen. Each child has a separate tray and eats with chopsticks. Today, the menu includes rice and fish, with a fresh satsuma for dessert.

Sun-Woo and her friends love to play hand-clapping games.

Family mealtime

Food plays a very important part in Korean family life. Every day, Sun-Woo and her family try to sit down together to eat and exchange news.

Sun-Woo loves the martial art of Tae Kwon Do and goes to classes three times a week.

Chiba's houses and factories sit on the long coastline of Tokyo Bay. The people who live there work in industries such as chemical production, fishing, and seaweed harvesting.

Momona from Japan

Momona is eight years old and lives in the city of Chiba, on the eastern coast of Japan. Her home is on the fifth floor of a large apartment block. She shares it with her mother, father, and younger sister and brother. Each day she takes the elevator to the ground, then walks with her friends to the nearby school.

Momona and Saaya head off to school

In the morning
Momona reads the children's section of the newspaper to find out about other children in the world. Then she leaves for school. There is a man-made stream outside her apartment that she likes to jump over.

Momona

Momona and her friend Kae ride unicycles (cycles with one wheel). Momona can also ride a bicycle.

Kae

School building
There are more than 600 children in Momona's school. The school has a library, gym, and outdoor swimming pool. In Momona's class, the children learn how to grow flowers and vegetables. Recently they grew sweet potatoes. Then they dug up, cooked, and ate them.

Shoe swap
There are rows and rows of cubby holes at the entrance to Momona's school. This is where Momona changes into her white indoor shoes, called *uwabaki*.

Class work

Momona sits at the front of the class, where she has a clear view. Momona likes school very much. Her favorite subjects include Japanese and music.

...I want to be a nice nursery school teacher and comfort small children when they cry.

At school children work in pairs on the computer, taking turns using the mouse.

Serving each other

The children work in teams, taking turns serving their classmates. They say *itadakimasu*—a prayer of thanks for the food. Then they sit down to eat in the classroom.

Lunch is tuna and rice, eaten using chopsticks. Momona drinks milk with this.

Clean sweep

Before she goes home, Momona and the other children clean the classroom. They wash and polish the floors, wipe the windows and lockers, and clean the sinks and restrooms. Momona likes having a clean classroom.

Keeping in shape

The children exercise in the large playground next to the school. They stretch, run, and climb on bars set up outside. Momona is very flexible and enjoys keeping in shape. For P.E. classes, children change into comfortable shorts and tops.

Children warm up by stretching.

Music lessons

Each week after school, Momona has a piano lesson. The teacher lives in Momona's apartment building and Momona goes to her home for classes.

Momona is learning about musical notes and practices writing them in her book.

At home

Momona and her four-year-old sister, Ririka, love making origami animals from paper. They made these frogs. When it is bedtime, the children unroll their mattresses, called futons, and sleep on them. The whole family sleeps in the same room.

Children all over Japan love Hello Kitty toys. Momona also loves her robotic dog. She would like to have a real dog one day.

Momona and her brother and sister share a futon for this photograph.

Junivio from East Timor

Junivio is 10 years old and lives in Maliana in East Timor, one of the poorest countries in Asia. His home has no electricity and there is no postal service to deliver letters. Junivio walks to the only school in the area, which is 20 minutes away.

This is Lorinko, Junivio's pet parrot.

In the family

Grandpa   Mom   Dad

Junivio lives with his mother, father, and grandfather. He has five brothers and sisters, and many cousins. Junivio also has a dog named Bonja, named after an Indian movie star.

Junivio with his brothers and cousins

Hot walk

Junivio walks past his favorite mountain every day on his way to school. He walks with his 11-year-old twin sisters, Lenah and Diana. Junivio wears his shirt outside his shorts because this helps him to keep cool in the hot and humid climate.

Class action

About 1,000 children go to Junivio's school, which is made up of three separate buildings. Junivio has classes in the afternoons, from 1 p.m. to 5 p.m. His favorite subject is math.

After school, Junivio plays tag with his brothers and sisters.

Junivio's sister and cousin cool down in a nearby stream.

The children work in groups guided by their principal. They do not use computers because the school does not have any.

Make it

Children do not make many art projects because the school has little money to pay for materials. However, Junivio's friend did make this drum from cardboard and colored paper.

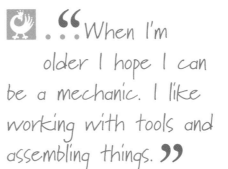

This drum makes a quiet thudding sound.

In class

There are 32 children in Junivio's class. They speak a mixture of the local language, Tetum, and Portuguese. Students wear either the blue school uniform or their usual clothes from home. Junivio likes everything about school and enjoys learning about new things.

Day-to-day

When it is dark, Junivio goes to sleep in the bedroom that is shared by the whole family. He does not want to be bitten by insects in the night, so he sleeps under a mosquito net.

Junivio is making a "number square" up to 100 so he can look for patterns in numbers.

Fix it

Junivio likes to take things apart and rebuild them. He spends hours working on his bike.

These wrenches are from Junivio's toolbox.

...When I'm older I hope I can be a mechanic. I like working with tools and assembling things.

Working at home

At home, Junivio practices math on his blackboard. He has one hour of homework each night. As there is no electricity at his home, he has to do it before the Sun sets, or by candlelight.

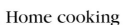

Home cooking

Junivio's mother is a school teacher. She also makes wonderful cakes and doughnuts dusted with powdered sugar. Her kitchen, at the back of the house, has a roof, but no walls. Junivio helps by collecting sticks for her wood-burning stove.

Team sports are not taught during class time at school, but the children play soccer during recess. At home, Junivio plays with boys from his village on the local soccer field. The village men play soccer matches here every week.

Children jump and dive into the water even though it is not deep.

The stream is a place to play, wash, and clean clothes.

Australasia

This consists of Australia, New Zealand, and several neighboring South Pacific islands. For the most part, teaching in Australia and New Zealand is in English, and schools are similar to European schools. At the same time, both countries have also developed schools where the language and traditions of the original population are taught.

This is Australasia

Australian kangaroo

The kangaroo is a symbol of Australia. As tall as a man, this vegetarian browser can really hop— up to 10 feet (3 meters) high.

Australian outback

The vast center of Australia, called the outback, consists of dry bushlands. Uluru, or Ayers Rock, (above) is in the Northern Territory. It is one of the oldest rocks on earth and was formed over a period of 500 million years.

PALAU

MICRONESIA

Rafting, New Zealand

Many New Zealanders enjoy adventure, like trips into the wilderness, bungy jumping, and white-water rafting (above). They also enjoy more traditional sports—rugby is the national sport, and cricket and netball are also popular.

Sydney, Australia

The sail shapes of the Sydney Opera House are world famous. Sydney is the most populated city in Australia. It is a harbor city and has many beautiful beaches.

PAPUA NEW GUINEA

SOLOMON ISLANDS

• **Yirrkala**

SAMOA

VANUATU

FIJI

NEW CALEDONIA
(To France)

TONGA

AUSTRALIA

A U S T R 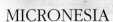 A L A S I A

Kiwi, New Zealand

The animal life in New Zealand is unique and exotic, and includes the kiwi bird—the national emblem of New Zealand.

Islands of New Zealand

There are two main islands, North and South, and the landscape ranges from craggy coastlines and long, sandy beaches to ancient forests and snow-capped mountains.

Turangi •

NEW ZEALAND

Great Barrier Reef, Australia

This is the greatest coral reef system in the world. It is so big that it can be seen from space. It supports amazingly varied sea life including turtles, humpback whales, sharks, clownfish, sea snakes, and giant clams.

Gapirri from Australia

Nine-year-old Gapirri lives in Yirrkala, Arnhem Land in the Northern Territory of Australia, with his father, two sisters, and two brothers. The community of just 1,000 people is famous for producing traditional Aboriginal art.

Aboriginal people have lived in Yirrkala since before historical records began.

Graham   Gloria   Rita   Timmy

Aaron

Aboriginal people use different names for different situations. It's common to use an Aboriginal name inside the community and a European name outside.

Yirrkala has a tropical climate and is warm all year round. Gapirri spends a lot of time on the beach.

SCHOOL

Cyclone-proof school
The school building has a modern look and is decorated with original works of art. It has been built to withstand a cyclone. Boys and girls are taught in separate classes.

Gapirri makes his way between the trees on the short walk to school.

Classes

Gapirri is in the fourth grade at school. Attendance is encouraged but not compulsory, so in order to appeal to the children, classes are informal, practical, and often take place outdoors. The children like to learn this way.

Classes are in Yolngu, the local language. The school day generally runs from 8:30 a.m. to 3 p.m., Monday to Friday.

Gapirri plays the drums and sings with his friends in a band. They practice at school, but the band doesn't have a name.

Playing basketball

Australian rules football is popular too.

...When we do corroboree (traditional dancing) I put white color on my face. It comes from a rock. You get a stick and crush it up and mix it with water.

Practical skills

The children often go on outings in the school bus. They practice archery in the bush. Most days, Gapirri also goes hunting with his father, Timmy, a ranger.

The beach

From his house, Gapirri can see the sea. He once saw a crocodile at the beach. School outings to a water hole or the beach are a chance to go fishing and swimming. Gapirri also goes to the beach with his father, who is teaching him how to spear, cook, and eat turtles. He's interested in becoming a ranger like his dad when he grows up.

Gapirri and his friends love diving for shells.

Imagine having this as your local playground!

On outings from school the children are taught to play safely.

Parekaawa from New Zealand

Parekaawa is 10 years old and lives in Turangi, on New Zealand's North Island. She is a member of the native Maori community and attends a bilingual school where both Maori and English are taught as well as Maori culture and traditions.

Family way
Parekaawa lives with her mother, father, and younger brother, Arekatera, near the shores of New Zealand 's largest lake, Lake Taupo. Parekaawa was named after a Maori princess by her grandmother and a close aunt.

In cooking, flax leaves are wrapped around raw food. The parcel is lowered into a hole over hot rocks and a damp cloth is placed on top to make it steam. Five hours later the food is ready.

Parekaawa plaits flax leaves to make flowers called puti-puti.

Flax flower

Nature walks
Some mornings, Parekaawa, Arekatera, and their dad go for walks to look at the hot pools and steaming streams that surround their home. In the forest they collect flax leaves, which they use in a traditional way of cooking.

School time
School starts at 8:30 a.m. Parekaawa travels there on a bus that sometimes breaks down. She and her friends wear a uniform with a swirling pattern on one side that represents local plant life. The triangle on the school emblem is a mountain.

Light touch

In class, Parekaawa learns about Maori carved totems called *poupou*. Parekaawa's teacher says that to enjoy and understand a carving properly, people have to look at it with their eyes open, then feel it with their eyes closed.

This is Parekaawa's father with her mother in his arms. The other figure is Arekatera.

Day-to-day

Parekaawa likes living near the lake and mountains because it is calm there. In summer she swims in the lake. In winter she goes skiing with her school.

Parekaawa calls her teacher "Whaea *Liz*." (Whaea means "auntie" or "elder").

Children help each other see and feel the carvings.

This carving is a junior boys' canoe-paddling trophy.

Parekaawa designs her own carving. It represents her family.

The haka *war dance* is performed in schools and on rugby fields by the New Zealand rugby team, the All Blacks.

At Brownies, Parekaawa cools off on a water slide. Water pours from a hose over a plastic sheet. Dish-washing liquid makes it slippery.

Traditional dancing

On special occasions children perform traditional Maori dances. The girls perform the *poi*, where they spin string balls in circles, and the boys perform the *haka*.

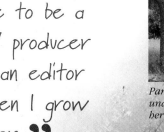

"...I would like to be a TV producer or an editor when I grow older."

Outside school Parekaawa keeps busy kicking a soccer ball, playing the piano, and going to a nearby Brownies group for girls.

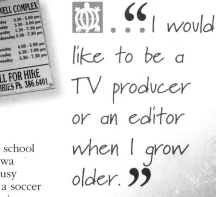

Parekaawa sits under a tree with her dad.

Index

Acknowledgments

Dorling Kindersley would like to thank all the staff at UNICEF who participated in this book, particularly: Katie Bucher, Julia Gorton (UK), Lisa Wolff, Francine Shelton (Canada), Iman Morooka (Egypt), Indrias Getachew (Ethiopia), Mmamiki Kamanakao, Othata Batsetswe, Jonathan Lewis (Botswana).
Thanks also to: Jay Goulden, Astrid Huerta Guevara, Care Huaraz (Peru), Jose Claudio Barros, Gilza Lopes Silveira de Mello, Priscilla Valdes, Patricia Magrini (Brazil), Gabriela Lopez Soria, Maria Cristina Galván Montero, Martin Furntes Chávez, Dr. Felipe Bracho Carpizo, María Elena Guerra y Sánchez, Conafe (Mexico), FIRST AIR, Kativik School Board (Canada), Clare and Tony Green (South Africa), Gina Fubini (Italy), Piotr Pininski (Poland), Inna Yakovleva (Russian Federation), Seda Darcan Ciftci (Turkey), AID-Delhi (India), Mr Chen Haiwen, Mr. Cui Xinhua (China), Hazel Benyon, The Venerable Baasansuren, VSO

office Ulaanbaatar (Mongolia), In-Joon Chung (South Korea), Mark Harris (East Timor), Timmy Burarrwanga (Australia). Also thanks to Ed Merritt for cartography.

The publisher would like to thank the following for their kind permission to reproduce their photographs:
(Key: a-above; b-below/bottom; c-center; f-far; l-left; r-right; t-top)
Alamy Images: AA World Travel Library 46tr; Caroline Cortizo 2cr; Karin Duthie 32tl; Chad Ehlers 51cr; Julio Etchart 51br; Gavin Hellier 25ca; Art Kowalsky 35tl (Ireland); Hideo Kurihara 51cra; Chris McLennan 52tr; Chris Pancewicz 35br; Photo Japan 71fcrb; Sepp Puchinger 30tl; Robert Harding Picture Library Ltd 25cra, 27tr (strawberry farm); Neil Setchfield 34cb (Tintin); Makoto Watanabe/MIXA Co., Ltd. 70tl; White Star / Monica Gumm 35fcrb; Anthony Wiles 35cl; **Bryan and Cherry Alexander Photography:** 53br, 53cr, 53crb, 53fcrb, 53l, 53tr, 53tr (children); **Corbis:** Jon Arnold/JAI 28tl; Tom Bean 9clb; Morton Beebe 9br; Bettmann 59tr; Dean Conger 51bc; Richard du Toit 26tr; Beat Glanzmann 9tl (dog sleigh); Chris Hellier 55cc; Joson 9cla; Bodh Kharbu 51bl; Wayne Lawler/Ecoscene 76tr; Charles & Josette Lenars 75ca; Gideon Mendel 26ca

(Nelson Mandela); Joseph Sohm/Visions of America 18tl; Paul A. Souders 25cr; Hubert Stadler 10tr; Eberhard Streichan 35fbr; Torleif Svensson 25br; Patrick Ward 40tl; Julia Waterlow/Eye Ubiquitous 28br; **Flickr.com:** mrfysla1 54c; taminator 9tr (ice hockey); **Getty Images:** altrendo travel 75br; Gary Bell 75bl; Ram Shergill 35fbl; VisionsofAmerica/Joe Sohm 38tr; **Photolibrary:** Charles Bowman/Robert Harding Picture Library Ltd. 68tr; **PunchStock:** Brand X Pictures 9fcra; Digital Vision 25bl; **Unicef:** 2bl, 3bl, 3c, 3cla, 3cra; Alenda Svirid 52bc, 52br
Jacket images: Front: **Corbis:** Angelo Cavalli/zefa c
All other images © Dorling Kindersley
For further information see: **www.dkimages.com**

And an extra big thanks to all the schools, staff, families, and especially the children, who appeared in *A School Like Mine.*

Thank you everyone.